Growing a Strong I

When parents belong to a minority religion such as Paganism, they rarely have the community support available to turn to when it comes time to involve their children in the rituals and activities that will teach them about Pagan beliefs.

This much-needed book will feed the hunger Pagan parents have to pass on their traditions and will help children share in the family's celebrations and perceptions, which will reinforce the family's Pagan identity. *The Pagan Family* is not just a book of rituals and information—it is full of opinions, arguments, and suggestions that address Pagans' real need to join in the quest for a form of Paganism that is alive and meaningful for children

The Pagan Family offers advice on the construction of rituals, and ritual guidelines for weddings, births, birthdays, seasonal celebrations, lunar phases, coming of age, divorce, and death ... suggestions for the creation of the sacred home, including blessings and household shrines ... activities for children such as meditating, mask and rattle making, drumming, and storytelling ... suggested prayers for throughout the day ... many tips for teaching children about Paganism ... and references and resources to lead Pagan parents to additional help.

Only out of the contending and complementing ideas of all Pagans will there eventually emerge a living Paganism for the next generation—and many to come.

"Practical, thorough, and plain-spoken, *The Pagan Family* widens the range of Craft family perspectives. It's especially sensitive and encouraging to parents with strong backgrounds in other religions, easing the transition to Pagan rites.

The Pagan Family integrates several cultural traditions into a non-denominational Pagan whole, with an engaging emphasis on folk-magic and custom. The rituals are beautiful and moving, and very powerfully connect us to the ancestral energies we all invoke."

—Ashleen O'Gaea
The Family Wicca Book

About the Author

Ceisiwr Serith has been a Pagan for seventeen years and a father for twelve. His background in Paganism includes working as a solitary, in small groups, and at Pagan gatherings. For the past twelve years he has been developing a system of Paganism that can be used by families. The result is a blend of the scholarly and the practical that is well-suited to the modern family.

Since 1985, Ceisiwr has been involved in the EarthSpirit Community, a group which organizes Pagan activities in the Boston area and New England. His articles have been published in *Circle Network News*, *EarthSpirit Community Newsletter*, and *Enchante*.

To Write to the Author

If you wish to contact the author or would like more information about this book, please write to the author in care of Llewellyn Worldwide, and we will forward your request. Both the author and publisher appreciate hearing from you and learning of your enjoyment of this book and how it has helped you. Llewellyn Worldwide cannot guarantee that every letter written to the author can be answered, but all will be forwarded. Please write to:

Ceisiwr Serith
c/o Llewellyn Worldwide
P.O. Box 64383-210, St. Paul, MN 55164-0383, U.S.A.

Please enclose a self-addressed, stamped envelope for reply, or $1.00 to cover costs. If outside the U.S.A., enclose international postal reply coupon.

Free Catalog from Llewellyn

For more than 90 years Llewellyn has brought its readers knowledge in the fields of metaphysics and human potential. Learn about the newest books in spiritual guidance, natural healing, astrology, occult philosophy, and more. Enjoy book reviews, new age articles, a calendar of events, plus current advertised products and services. To get your free copy of *Llewellyn's New Worlds of Mind and Spirit*, send your name and address to:

Llewellyn's New Worlds of Mind and Spirit
P.O. Box 64383-210, St. Paul, MN 55164-0383, U.S.A.

The Pagan Family

Handing the Old Ways Down

Ceisiwr Serith

1994
Llewellyn Publications
St. Paul, Minnesota 55164-0383, U.S.A.

FIRST EDITION
First Printing, 1994

Cover painting by Clyde Duensing III
Interior illustrations and photos by Ceisiwr Serith and Linda Norton
Book design and layout by Trish Finley

Library of Congress Cataloging-in-Publication Data
Serith, Ceisiwr, 1957-
    The pagan family : handing the old ways down / Ceisiwr Serith.
       p.   cm.
    Includes bibliographical references and index.
    ISBN 0-87542-210-1
    1. Paganism. 2. Family—Religious life. 3. Witchcraft. 4. New Age movement. 5. Rites and ceremonies. 6. Religious education—Home training. I. Title.
BL625.6.S47   1994
299—dc20   93-48689
                                          CIP

Llewellyn Publications
A Division of Llewellyn Worldwide, Ltd.
P.O. Box 64383, St. Paul, MN 55164-0383

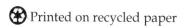 Printed on recycled paper

For
Debbie and Elizabeth

Contents

Foreword

I started writing this book a few years ago, but I have been working on it for the thirteen years I have been married, especially the twelve I have been a father. During that time I have been working out what it means to raise Pagan children and to practice Paganism with them. This has required a lot of original work; there were no books specifically on this subject that I could turn to. A lot of my time was spent writing and trying out rituals; indeed, the creation, performance, acceptance, modification, or rejection of rituals has been an important part of this book's genesis. The rituals my family has rejected could make their own book.

The problems that face my family are not unique. As the young Pagan movement starts to leave its adolescent years behind and its members raise children, the problems become more acute. Are we to remain a religion of converts? Or will we be able to develop an organic form of Paganism in our children, one that is as much a part of them as their names, one that will grow when we are no longer here to feed it? The answers are at least two generations away. New cultures take time. We will not know whether we have been successful until our grandchildren are grown, but it is time to start.

This is a book for families with children. These are not the only kinds of families, of course, but there are already a number of books that can be used by families composed of adults. The kind of Paganism that works with adults doesn't necessarily work with children. A different kind of Paganism is required, and that is what I have concentrated on. For the purpose of this book, therefore, I have defined family as a multi-generational group of people, one or more of whom are children, living together or possessing a close tie of blood or love.

In a sense no Pagan is without children. We are all responsible for the rearing of the next generation. The old myths tell us this, with the uncles, aunts, and grandparents that serve as teachers. Our own experiences as children tell us this, with many of us having better relationships with our grandparents than our parents. And now, as adults, it is our turn to teach the world's children, even if none of them have sprung from us, even if none of them even live in our house.

This brings us to the thorny question of what a Pagan can teach another's child. The lessons of honesty, fairness, respect for others and for the planet—these we can teach with enthusiasm. But what of our Pagan ways? How much of that can be passed on?

The answer to this is simple to formulate but hard to accept. As long as a child is legally under the care of others you must get permission from those people before you teach anything about religion. Perhaps it can be made easier to accept if you imagine how you would feel if someone else's parents tried to save your child's soul.

There is still plenty of ambiguity here. For instance, can you tell myths? Be careful, but yes, it is possible. If you know the children's parents are Fundamentalists, even this is dangerous. Be careful. We do not do ourselves or Paganism any favors if we make others afraid that we will try to steal their children's souls. If there is any doubt at all, refrain.

That having been said, I would like to extend an invitation to Pagans who do not have children of their own to help those of us who do. It is a hard thing to raise Pagan children in our culture, and we can certainly use the help. When our children reach their difficult teenage years (do not be under the illusion that Pagan children will somehow have an easy adolescence), they will need adults other than their parents to confide in and seek advice. And let me say it again—we all have children. Our children belong to the People, and the next generation is everyone's business.

This is not just a book of rituals and information. There is no Neo-Pagan authority to give final judgements or to impose liturgy. Here you will find opinions, arguments, and suggestions. You may disagree with some of them. Your vision of Paganism may be very different. If it is, please add your voice to the discussion. The Paganism of the future will have many roots. Out of the contending and complementing of ideas will eventually come a living Paganism for the next generation and the next. After that, they're on their own.

Although I have intended to provide a complete system of Family Paganism, this book is more than that. It is an invitation to Pagans to join in the quest for a form of Paganism that can mean something to our children. That is why as well as including rituals for occasions I have pointed the way towards developing your own rituals, both in the "traditions to raid" sections and in the references and resources. These are as important a part of the book as the set rituals. This is as it should be. Paganism is a tree, not a crystal; it will continue to grow and change as long as earth and sky endure.

I have written mainly for the reader who is already familiar with Paganism, but I have included some basic information for the non-Pagan who may have seen this book and thought, "A Pagan family? What the heck does that mean?" With the great variety within Paganism of both practice and belief this information may also come in handy for Pagans who want to know what sort of Pagan wrote this, as well as adding to the growing body of Pagan theology. There is a glossary of terms that may be unfamiliar to some readers.

The major source I looked to in devising these rituals was the culture of the British Isles. This delightful mix of Celtic, pre-Celtic, Roman, Anglo-Saxon, Viking, Christian, and who knows what, is not only the source for most Neo-Paganism (through the influence of Wicca, the most popular form of Neo-Paganism). It is also a perfect example of just how well syncretism can work. Since most Americans have at least some ancestors from the British Isles (or from their cousins in the Germanic and Celtic regions of northern

Europe), and since so much of American culture is already based on their cultures, much will seem familiar.

Three other cultures made major contributions. First, I have found Roman religion and folk custom to have much to offer. They are well-documented, presenting a virtually complete Pagan Indo-European culture. They were especially useful in developing rituals for the house and its guardians, as well as setting the tone for many of the other rituals. Much of Roman religion took place in the home and is thus especially relevant here. And, in typical Pagan fashion, what they did was more important to them than what they believed. Indeed, there were numerous traditions they did not understand the reason for, but still they kept them. They knew how to remember. And they have left their mark on Western popular culture, so their customs seem natural, like old friends. Roman influence has already entered Neo-Paganism through Wicca, both directly through the classical educations of its founders (or revivers, depending on which version of the myth of the origin of Wicca is believed), and indirectly, through the effects of Roman culture on British folk custom both during the conquest and after.

The Native American cultures also made a major contribution to my book. While they had no effect on the origins of Neo-Paganism, in America they began to influence Pagans early on. This influence has increased in recent years and may even be crossing the Atlantic. (I have heard that English Pagans have rediscovered drumming.) Native American cultures were important both in filling the gaps left by my other sources and in answering the question of what this land asks of us. While many Native Americans see Neo-Pagans as pillaging their cultures, we must still look to them for inspiration. Who else can teach us how to live on this continent in a way that will satisfy earth and sky?

Lastly, I found Judaism to be a source of inspiration. After the destruction of the Temple and the scattering of their people, Jews found they had no choice but to keep their religion alive in their homes. As a minority religion subject to persecution they have kept the way of their ancestors strong through two thousand years. If we do only half as well, we will have cause for pride.

Many other cultures, from all the continents of the world, have made their marks on this book. I have tried to choose with respect and not merely plunder. If any readers feel their culture has been misrepresented, I apologize in advance and ask that they write and educate me.

Because Paganism reveres female and male equally, Pagans are concerned about sexist language. In particular, we want to avoid the generic "he." However, since Pagans revere both the spoken and the written word, we are also concerned about both clarity and beauty of expression.

Sometimes these concerns clash. Some of the alternatives to the general use of "he" are awkward (constant use of "he or she" is annoying) and some are unpronounceable and therefore distracting to many readers. (I am thinking here of constructions such as s/he.) The problem can be avoided in many cases by putting sentences in the passive mode, using plural verbs, or avoiding pronouns. Sooner or later, though, an author encounters a situation where none of these will work.

When I have encountered these situations in this book I have tried to balance the needs of non-sexism, clarity, and beauty. What I have mostly done is to use either "he" or "she," choosing in a somewhat random manner. (As the father of a daughter, I must confess a tendency to write of children as "she.") Where either sex is specifically meant, this will be obvious from context.

Most of these rituals can be performed with a minimum of equipment. With the exception of the wedding, dedication of a baby, and funeral (which require the usual Wiccan tools), the items needed are likely to be around your house already or easily acquired, items such as bowls, bells, candles, and flowers. Rattles and drums are less common than bowls, perhaps, but they're not rare in Pagan households.

The items you use may be as special as a Wiccan's athame, her ritual knife. They may be special in a different way, like china used only on holidays. Or they may be ordinary things, special by virtue of being the materials of everyday life.

Many people helped this book along its way. The reference section gives the names of some of them. Special thanks are due to Beth Goldstein, who first said, "You should write a book." Patricia Telesco, who reviewed my original manuscript for Llewellyn, made many good suggestions. Her critique taught me a lot about writing and helped turn a rough work into a finished one. John Yohalem, editor of *Enchante*, made many good suggestions regarding Chapter 3. The EarthSpirit Community provided support and guidance, as well as teaching me much of what I know about ritual. And of course, my wife and daughter were vital to this book's creation. As well as putting up with my clumsy early efforts at ritual construction, they proofread, made suggestions, and taught me about family dynamics. My daughter taught me how to make gods' eyes, and made sure my directions were correct.

❦ 1 ❧

Introduction to Paganism

Paganism is not a thing of the past. It has survived years of neglect and persecution, and is now returning to life. It has spent a long time in hidden corners of the world, or sleeping beneath a thin blanket of Christianity in the folk customs of country people. But now it is waking up. It is a beautiful day, and Neo-Pagans—those of us who are reviving the old ways—are glad to see it.

Neo-Paganism is diverse, drawing its inspirations from many cultures. Its practitioners range from people pouring out libations on the beach, to shamans riding their drumbeats to the spirit world, to Wiccans practicing complex rites involving special tools and knowledge. I cannot speak for the details of all of its forms. They are as varied as the people who practice them. But its spirit, its principles, its attitude toward the world—these all Pagans share, and of them I can speak.

Pagans live in this world, recognizing it as sacred. We do not see it as merely a temporary thing, nor as the manifestation of something of greater sacredness. There is no other world that is more real and of more value than this. We are not mere sojourners here, marking time until we can die and go to the real and eternal world. This is our world; we belong here and we like it that way.

When I walk outside each morning I feel as if I belong. This is my planet and I am part of it as surely as my fingers are part of me. The sky is above me, the earth is below me, and I walk in between, accepted and loved.

When I walk in the woods, I feel the individual personalities of each tree and stone. When I walk in the city I feel the complex patterns of power woven by so many people. Either place I am at home. This is my planet and these are my people.

Pagans are great workers of rituals. No matter how complex or ornate these rituals may be, however, they are not an escape from the world. We use them to celebrate the world and to adjust ourselves and our lives to harmonize with the world.

The material world fills our rituals. We orient our rituals and our lives by the four directions. The four classical elements, or types of matter (air, fire, water, and earth), are our constant reference. The most common symbol used by Neo-Pagans is the pentagram, adopted from ceremonial magic. This five-pointed interlaced star is the symbol for a reality formed of the weaving together of the elements with spirit. Matter and spirit are not separate, but interdependent. Most ritual actions are performed clockwise (Pagans call it deosil) to mimic the motion of sun and moon in the sky. Offerings to our deities are of everyday items, particularly food and drink.

Don't misunderstand me; Pagans are quite interested in the sacred. But it is a sacred which is not opposed to the profane. We may make a space sacred for a ritual, but it is the same space as before and will be the same space after. For a time, though, we are more aware of its sacredness, more attentive. The ritual helps us to remember its sacredness. "Remember" is an important word to us.

Paganism is not a religion of metaphysical dualism. Matter is not opposed to, or even separate from, spirit. Nor is the material, the everyday, somehow not fitting for religious purposes. The earth and all its delights is as sacred as those things normally considered "spiritual."

Nor are Pagans ethical dualists. Evil does not exist as a force or a personality. Many of the disasters that beset us (floods, tornadoes, disease) are disasters only from the human point of view. But our Mother and Father have many children, and most are not human beings. The disease that kills me may be the result of millions of bacteria being allowed to live. This is hard on me and I don't like it, and I certainly have the right to fight the disease, but it isn't evil. It is part of the great dance of life and death.

The terrible things that humans do are no proof of evil either. When examined closely, they are seen to be unbalanced forms of very positive things—the aggression that helped win us our place in evolution, the sexuality that continues our species, the loyalty to family and community that gives us our strength. It is a terrible thing when such wonderful forces are carried to bad ends. The term "sacrilege" comes to mind. But it does not show the existence of an evil force, nor does it challenge the existence or power of the gods.

The emphasis on this world does not mean that for the Pagan it is the only world. In fact, there is a different world existing in close connection with ours. This is the Otherworld, the Land of Youth, the Dreamtime, the home of the Ancestors, the Land of Faerie. It is the home of gods and spirits, the source of numinous power. It sometimes seems far away, but it is actually right here, existing with ours. Where else would it be?

Be careful next time you wander in the fog; you may wander into the Land of Faerie. Perhaps the greatest mystery of Paganism is that if the Pagan path is followed with dedication the two worlds approach each other more closely, until the Pagan lives in both at once. This is one way a Pagan sees the sacredness of our world.

Perhaps you are thinking, "What does all this sacred world stuff have to do with Paganism? I thought Pagans were simply people who believe in more than one god." Of course we do; it says so right in the dictionary. We do not believe that the infinite variety we see around us can be attributed to the action of one sacred being. There is immense variety on the material level, and we believe there is equally immense variety on the spiritual.

For this reason, the numinous beings of Paganism are many. They can be as far-reaching as the One that we all are (humans and the rest of the Universe as well). They can be as local as the spirit of a rock, limited in time and space. And there are many gradations in between: the God and Goddess, deities of particular cultures, ancestral spirits, family guardians, power animals—the list is practically endless. While not every Pagan would choose to work with all of these, most Pagans would accept their validity.

Almost all Neo-Pagans revere the Goddess and God. They are the Mother and Father of All; from their love new worlds are continually born. The Goddess is the origin of being, the power behind the Universe, the bringer into manifestation. She goes by many names, and of these the most popular among Neo-Pagans are Diana and Isis. I myself call Her "Maghya," which is Proto-Indo-European for "She Who Has the Power" and that she certainly has. The God is the one who acts, the wielder of power, the one who is the masks that reveal the Universe. His most popular name among Neo-Pagans is Cernunnos, which means "The One with the Antlers," for He is frequently depicted wearing those symbols of maleness and wildness.

The God and Goddess are protectors and teachers and, like human parents, they must occasionally discipline their children. They love all their children equally and expect them to treat each other as family. They are our role models as parents.

The fact that Pagans worship a divine that does not exclude the female has caught many people's attention. Although at some theological level the God of the religions of the West may be said to be without gender, the ways in which this God has been conceived have been almost exclusively male. That Neo-Paganism celebrates male and female equally has certain effects on Pagan family life. Neo-Pagan families are likely to avoid sexual stereotypes, and to encourage excellence in both boys and girls.

On the other hand, we recognize essential differences between the sexes. But since our divinities are both male and female these differences are not differences in worth. We welcome and celebrate the differences.

Since this book is written for families, not covens, groves, congregations, or mystics, the spiritual beings called upon will tend toward the lower end of the range, the local spirits that shape our mundane lives. The One is best left to individual attention. God and Goddess will not be forgotten, but they too are well left for the individual, or for the coven or other group. Their great mysteries of love and sex are not always appropriate in a family setting. The main inspirations for family Paganism are folk traditions, the everyday customs and the special day customs of the common people. Its deities are the comfortably worn down and worn in ones of the European peasant: the Threshold Guardian, Hearth Guardian, spirits of the dead, spirits of the wild, and such. The

Shining Ones have their times, and they will be honored here, but a family can concern itself with the household spirits and flourish.

The beings of power, the gods, exist not only on a continuum of power, but of space and time. Every place and moment is filled with them. They can be found by all who open themselves to them.

Sometimes I encounter the gods. Sometimes I feel a quiver, like a whisper or a breeze that just makes itself known without giving more information. Have you ever felt an itch and not known where it was coming from? The gods can come like that, a Cosmic Itch.

Sometimes they are inside me. Cernunnos comes with strength when I am weak and courage when I am scared. He fills me; I am taller and larger and more muscular. From my head antlers reach up, pulling me up and weighing me down. He is there, and he helps me.

Sometimes they are right here in front of me. I see them, I hear them; they are there and they are helping me. They are there, and I make no apologies for that belief.

And sometimes it is not them but their effects I feel. I am surrounded by their love when I am lonely. I am comforted when I am troubled. And I am given help when I need it.

The gods are there, in the way of the world, the living and dying that makes our planet. The wind, the waves, the stone and the tree reveal the sacred.

When I see the dying of the year, I mourn with it. This mourning is itself a source of strength, for while I may mourn with the death of the year, I will rejoice in its rebirth. All this drama is played out within me.

So when I face my own death I do it with a little less fear and a little more comfort. I have seen the earth die and be reborn and I know that I am indeed part of this earth. I too will be reborn, not because I have an immortal soul that is living innumerable lifetimes to learn its way to godhood (although that might be true, and who am I to say yes or no?), but because this is my home. This is where I was born. I grew from the earth and there is nowhere else I belong. Not only can you go home again; there is no place else you can go.

I know that I am a part of all this, a part of the turning and changing that is our world. I live now, I will die then, and the world will go on. I will have done my part and I pray I will have done it well. No one else could have done it.

But when I am gone, I will have left an effect behind. Everyone I meet will have been changed by me, just as I was changed by them. Everything I have consumed will have left my mark, for good or bad. Nothing, though, will have left as large an effect as how I raised my daughter, how she came to see the world, and how she went on to affect it in turn.

Despite these wonderful feelings, Paganism is not about feeling. It is about *doing*. A Pagan is someone who walks a Pagan path. She aligns her life with the seasons and the moons, treats the planet gently, and shows respect to the others who share our world, to minerals, plants, animals, people, spirits, and deities.

It is for this reason that many Pagans are fond of saying that "Paganism is not just a religion, it's a way of life." This can come across as snobbery, as if other religions weren't serious enough, but it should be taken literally. Paganism is a way of life, or perhaps it would be more correct to say it is a way of living. What do you do? That will tell you if you are Pagan.

Watch the world. Learn from it. Learn what you have to do to live in balance with its ways. Listen to the world. Hear its voice. It speaks to you in rhythm.

Go to where Pagans gather and you will feel the rhythm. Listen to the drums. They start spontaneously, all sizes and types, and the rhythm grows and changes. The people dance to them. Listen carefully and you will hear your own rhythms—heartbeat, breath, sleeping and waking, menstruation, life and death and rebirth.

Turn then from your own rhythms. Turn from the rhythms of the drumming and dancing of the community. Turn to the world about you and feel her rhythms. Live these rhythms: day and night, moon change, season flow.

And in the flow, something will seem right. There, on the edge of your mind, is a tickling of memory, like déjà vu. Was it in another life? Or is it just part of being human? Something tells you: Remember. So you try. It says: Remember the stories of your ancestors. Remember those who died for you. Remember that this world is your home. Remember and things will be OK.

The rituals in this book are here to help you and your children remember. When the old deeds are done, when the old songs are sung, the mind remembers, the body remembers. Do you want to understand Paganism? Do the rituals—and remember.

❦ 2 ❧

Ritual

A ritual is a "coherent set of symbolic actions that has a real, transformative effect on individuals and social groups" (Lincoln, p. 6). Rituals give (or reveal) meaning to the moments and actions with which they are associated.

Ritual is the heart and soul of Paganism. It is the sacred acting through which we celebrate the world and gods. By taking part in ritual we are not only learning how to live rightly; to perform the rituals is to live rightly. There are rituals of time, when we do what is most appropriate for a given moment, and rituals of place, when we do what is most appropriate for a given location. We perform them at the right time and at the right place and thereby act rightly. And Pagans are what they do.

Some rituals are unlearned. Mankind seems to have an innate genius for developing and elaborating rituals. They spring out of us when the moment calls for them. But if a ritual is to go beyond a small group of people it must be learned. The symbolic acts it is composed of make up a language which must be understood by those who will perform it, and this language must be learned.

This is one reason why Pagans study the old stories, why we make lists of gods and goddesses and their corresponding attributes and rituals. We are teaching ourselves a ritual language with which to communicate with each other, with nature, and with the sacred.

The form and purpose of a ritual is affected by the number and type of people who are performing it. Covens frequently concentrate on magic, individuals may spend long periods in meditation, and large groups often employ sacred drama. A family, though, is a special case. It is a small group, but some of its members are children. That changes everything.

Neo-Paganism in America has become almost synonymous with Wicca, the British religion developed in the middle of this century by Gerald Gardner and Doreen Valiente. Wicca's years in this country have affected it greatly, and although it still exists in private covens it is also found in open Pagan communities. These communities draw some basic assumptions about ritual and religion from Wicca, and unfortunately some of those don't work when children are involved.

Wicca is a Mystery Religion. As such, some of its rites are performed in secret by initiates, with mysteries that can only be understood by undergoing rituals. It is strongly influenced by ceremonial magic. The rituals involve a heavy symbolism that has to be learned before the rituals make sense. Wicca grew in small groups of adults and its ritual structure reflects that.

A mistake often made by Pagan parents is to bring the children into Wiccan rituals or, at the least, to compose rituals based closely on what is done by a coven. This arises from a misunderstanding of the role of Mystery Religions in culture.

In a living Pagan culture, there are several levels of involvement. There may be Mystery Religions or secret societies (or there may not), but they are not the whole story. There are also public rites, folk traditions, superstitions, spirits of the land, mealtime customs—the list is long. The rituals in the home are not the public rituals, nor are they the mystery rituals.

In pre-Christian days Pagans lived in Pagan communities. When Christianity came, the individual and family rites frequently disappeared. What showed the most staying power were the practices of the entire community, Christianized and secularized, but still recognizably pre-Christian.

Many folk customs are only appropriate for communities. If you are a member of a Neo-Pagan community of families, you are a lucky person indeed. Your children will benefit immeasurably from feeling that they are not total weirdoes and realizing that there are other Pagan children and that you're not making all this up. You will benefit from this support as well.

But most of us struggle along alone. This book was written for these people, adapting as much of the community rituals for the family as possible and regretfully leaving out what could not be. I will at times give suggestions for those with a community, but the emphasis had to be on those families who were alone. If you are one of the lucky ones, please go to the sources and bring back as much as you can. We will all be enriched thereby.

The rituals in this book have therefore been written with a nuclear family in mind. One or two adults and children—that is the family I had in mind when I wrote these. If your family is larger, that is wonderful. It is especially wonderful if it includes three or more generations. There are provisions in this book for stretching the rituals, but in general I had to write for the minimum. It is easier to adapt from this to a larger group than the other way round. As long as the number of people involved doesn't get much higher than a dozen, these rituals will work.

Most of the time in these rituals the roles taken by adults can just as well be taken by either men or women. In some cases, though, it seemed that one or the other was most fitting. For instance, it would have been a shame to throw out hundreds, perhaps thousands, of years of having a May Queen, and it seemed only right that a Full Moon ritual should be presided over by a woman, as representative of the Goddess. Where a ritual specifies a man or a woman, then there is a good reason for it.

Can you do these rituals another way? Most certainly. If you have a single-parent family, you will have to. This is a principle found in other religions as well; in Judaism, for example, it is standard for the mother to light the Sabbath candles. If there is no mother, an adult woman may do it, and if there is no adult woman, than a man may. Better that than leave them unlit. A man taking a woman's part in a ritual is not a breach of tradition. For this to happen is itself part of the tradition, and those who do it this way are not performing second-class rituals. They are following the old ways.

In general, it is best to establish a pattern and not vary from it without good reason. Traditions are very important to children; doing things the same way means the world is safe. There will still be times when you will have to do things differently, when a family member is sick, for instance.

You may wish to assign roles differently than I have as a rule. That is certainly your right. To tell the truth, in my own family some of the rituals are done differently than the way they are given in this book; I take the mother's parts in the Full Moon observance, for instance. The only rituals where a man cannot take the woman's part or a woman the man's, are the puberty rituals. Only a man can make a man, and only a woman can acknowledge a woman.

Pagans are used to following their instincts when it comes to ritual. Personal intuition is not only allowed, it is encouraged. The key phrase is, "as long as it works."

Families will find themselves doing this as well. As your family develops its identity and personality, you will find the rituals you use being modified. This is not unique to Paganism, of course; next time you're with some Christian friends ask them when they put their Christmas trees up.

Since you are working with a family there will, however, be less room for personal intuition. Bluntly put, no one person has a right to make a major change in a family ritual. Fine-tuning, tweaking, and knob-twiddling are fine. You will find this especially necessary the first time you do a ritual.

But a major change in something that has been done before with children will defeat the whole purpose of family religion. What will it teach your children? That this is your religion, not theirs; that there is no certainty to the cycles being celebrated; that you do not consider religion or them important enough to subdue your momentary impulses. Tread carefully when making changes.

On the other hand, your children will make changes of their own, frequently in the middle of a ritual. If these changes are not in keeping with the spirit of the ritual, you will have to say nicely, "No, we do things another way." You are the adult, and you are the teacher, and one of the things you need to teach is that sometimes we can't let what we want take precedence over the wishes of others.

Usually, though, the changes will be just fine. These are to be enthusiastically adopted. They give a ritual meaning for the child who makes them, and the fact that you go along with them shows the child that her opinions are valued. The very fact that she cares to make changes at all is a good sign; it shows that she is making Paganism her own.

Traditions that you have yourself grown up with will have a comfortable feel to them that ones you found in a book (including this one) will not. Children know when you feel self-conscious about something and will in turn feel uncomfortable themselves. Traditions take a while to wear down around the edges.

Don't be afraid to adapt customs you are used to, even if they are non-Pagan. While some are religious in origin and form, many others are secular. Some are both. Bells at Christmas, for instance, come from both church bells and sleigh bells. Adopt, adapt, reinterpret. Cultures have always done this, Pagan as well as Judeo-Christian.

It is a time-honored tradition for religions to steal customs from each other. For example, Neo-Pagans stole jumping over a broomstick at weddings from the Gypsies who stole it from the peasants of the Netherlands and northern Germany. Stolen traditions don't stay unchanged by the theft. The tree stolen from Pagans by Christians became a Christmas tree. If we now steal it back in its changed form we will ourselves change it. That's OK.

To help creative stealing, I have included traditions to raid in some of the chapters. Information on them can be found in the books listed in the references. These traditions are holidays from other ways that parallel Neo-Pagan observances in some sense. Investigate them carefully, and if you find something which will enrich your celebration, adopt and adapt it with respect. These are not just hoards to plunder. They are places to find answers to the questions of how people respond to the world. Don't look to them only for customs, but for what they tell you about what it is to be human.

Rituals can have a variety of structures. They can be dramas, declarations, litanies, dances—the list is long. The language used can have a variety of styles as well. It can be Elizabethan, romantic, blunt—an equally long list. Which style a family should use is based both on personal preference and the maturity of the children.

Let's face it, no matter how exalted Elizabethan English sounds to you, all it will teach a seven year old is that religion is boring. So drop the "thee's" and "thou's" and drop expressions like "We do bless you." People just don't talk like that and children just won't listen to it.

Your words don't have to be flat, however. Try rhyme, or, if your rhymes are like mine and keep ending up sounding like greeting cards, use alliteration. That was the original poetic form of English. Say the words out loud before using them in a ritual. Do they flow smoothly? Do they fit with each other? Are there any words that when put next to each other sound stupid? ("The nether lands," for instance.) Are all the sentences of the ritual in the same style? Are they simple enough for your children to understand? Most of all, do they mean what you really want them to, with no unintended ambiguity?

It is in keeping with the spirit of Paganism that the words are optional. You may say them before or after the act that accompanies them, or eliminate them altogether. The words in the rituals in this book move me or I wouldn't have written them, but it is the actions that are important. Sometimes the mind seizes words like a life preserver—"Oh good, something I understand." Then the action does not cut to the heart. Words are good for explanations. Actions are good for rituals. Do the deeds. Do what your ancestors did. Stand in their place.

Some of these rituals have relatively long declarations. Instead of one person doing them, they could be broken up among family members. This will allow more participation if your family is large. They could be put in question and answer form. This will involve the family members more than simple speeches by the parents.

One cruel truth about children: they don't like to listen to a lot of words. They fidget. They ask questions that have nothing to do with what's going on. They turn their bodies to jelly and slide off their chairs.

There are things they do like, however. As a Pagan parent your job will be much easier if you do the things they like. OK, you can slip in your own things too, but make a sandwich with the kids' things as the bread.

First, they like celebrations. They like parties, presents, and decorations. Celebrations are perfect for Seasonal Festivals and Rites of Passage.

Kids like to do things. The same child that went glassy-eyed at your reading of the Charge may gladly read it herself and will feel thrilled about it. Since Paganism is a religion of doing, give your children something to do. Have them carry something, move something, say something. The first time our family celebrated Brighid's Day our daughter took over the ritual. She took the cross and insisted on saying the words in each room by herself.

Kids like to sing. Paganism has lots of songs. Pagan magazines carry advertisements for recordings. (The names of some recordings are given in the reference section.) Buy some, play them, and sing them. Songs can keep the power to move long after the religion they belong to has been left behind. Christmas songs still get to me after almost twenty years as a Pagan. Such is the power of songs.

Listen to your children. They will let you know what is working and what isn't. This listening requires great subtlety. A child may "act cool" about something that really matters to him. He may groan when you start to tell a myth and then be drawn in by it and start asking questions about what happened next. He may complain about having to do a ritual but remind you if you forget to do it. He may fidget when meditating with you and then you find him meditating on his own. Watch carefully and see what catches fire. Don't give up after one try.

Each ritual with children (like rituals with adults) should include the standard and the special, what Catholics call the Ordinary and the Proper. The standard is the frame which tells participants that a ritual is being done and that puts the rest of the ritual in the appropriate context of the religious tradition. The special is the part that conveys the message of the particular ritual. In writing the seasonal rituals (Chapter 7), I tried to devise something for each festival that would be unique to it, something that hopefully would capture a child's imagination and make her look forward to the day. Something special—something that tells your children that they are a part of a religion of beauty, awe, and fun—is what will keep Paganism alive in them.

The standard part of the ritual is just as important, however. The fact that it is repeated says that our way is one of reassurance, that it is as steady as the yearly cycles it celebrates, that we are not just making it up as we go along. Our way turns, but it turns back to its beginning.

One of the characteristics that Neo-Paganism has inherited from Wicca is a preoccupation with sacred space. In part this is a result of the influence of ceremonial magic, in which a sacred space, a "magic circle," is necessary to keep the magician safe from the spirits he has called up. In Wicca the meaning of the circle changed to a means of keeping power in until it is required.

In general, a family practicing Paganism in their home has no need to create sacred space before a ritual. The home should already have been made sacred ritually by blessing it, but even more important, a home is made sacred by the very fact that a family lives in it. The daily activities of a family are sacred acts, and they continually consecrate the place where they are performed. The home is the temple, and the family table the altar.

When a ritual is performed outside the home, however, or when it involves a large number of people who are not family members (or both), creation of sacred space is a good idea. The rituals in this book that are likely to need sacred space to be created include directions specific to them. However, perhaps a bit of general theory will help make more sense of these directions.

Neo-Pagan sacred space is generally circular (although practical considerations may sometimes require a different shape). For this reason, the ritual for creating it is called "casting the circle." The meanings of this shape are many, and all of them can be implied by its use.

For instance, circles are symbols of eternity, since they never end. They symbolize wholeness, since they represent a pattern returning to the beginning. The circle is the strongest shape. It represents the natural cycles that we are celebrating; the year, the moon, menstruation, life and death and rebirth, night and day. It is what we tend to think of when we think of a hole, and thus the most appropriate shape for a conduit between the sacred and profane worlds.

Perhaps the greatest reason for using a circle, though, comes from its geometric characteristics. When we stand in the center of a circle, we are the same distance from each point on its rim. In the same way, we each stand in the center of the universe, and in the center of the visible world; we are exactly halfway from horizon to horizon. In this way the circle represents the world.

A second characteristic of a circle is that no one section of it is shaped differently from any other. In this way, the equal worth of the four directions, the four elements, and all of their corresponding qualities is affirmed.

The first step in casting a circle is to delineate it. We must know where our circle ends, both spiritually and physically. It may be marked physically with just about anything. Popular choices are rocks, flowers, rope, chalk, or poles. These are laid out in a clockwise direction, starting in the east (where the sun rises) or the north (the darkness out of which everything is born). The size marked out will vary based on the number of people who must fit into the circle.

The physical marking out may be done before the ritual if necessary. However, it is more in keeping with the properly Pagan belief in the sacredness of the material to make the physical marking part of the ritual. The circle is thereby blessed in the very act of its physical creation.

After the circle is marked, it must then be consecrated in a more obviously spiritual manner. This is generally done by circling it reciting ritual words such as:

> *Blessed be this circle*
> *where we will perform great deeds.*
> *May it be a suitable place*
> *for our meeting with the gods.*

(This circling is sometimes given the marvelous name of "circumambulation.") While the circling is done, the celebrant may sprinkle blessed water, or carry incense, a lit candle, or a sacred tool such as an athame, wand, or rattle. More than one of these may be done. The minimum requirement, however, is one circling with words that may be done at the same time as the physical marking.

After the blessing of the border of the circle, the four directions are honored. In some traditions, this is called invoking the Guardians of the Watchtowers. These traditions tend to personify the directions and call the personified spirits of them. Other possibilities are to call the elements associated with the directions (air for east, fire for south, water for west, and earth for north) or the four winds. More simply, the celebrant can say:

> *May the spirits of the* (direction) *be with us here*
> *to bless us in all we do today.*

More specific words are given with each of the rituals that require them.

Candles are frequently placed at the four directions. They are lit as each of the directions is called on. For night rituals you will most likely want more candles for the purpose of illumination, but these should not be lit until after the circle is cast, or the lighting of the directional ones will be overshadowed.

When used outside, candles will have to be in jars except on the calmest of days. Many stores sell outdoor candles or tiki torches which work very well in the summer. They are especially nice in large gatherings where candles would be too small.

Once all the candles are lit, the circle is cast, and the rest of the ritual may start.

When sacred space is not created at the beginning of a ritual, there is still a need for a clear start. After the family is gathered together for a ritual there is often an awkward moment of waiting. There is too often a lot of looking at each other, thinking or saying, "Should we begin now?" The beginning of the rite needs a clear break from this moment. What is needed is a clear indication that sacred time has begun. Instead of creating sacred space, then, create sacred time.

There are many ways to do this. I have found that the best is with sound, particularly a special sound, used for nothing else. Sounds exist in time in a special way, arising and then dying off. Making a sound is a divider between times; when it is first made, the sound dissolves the previous time, and when it dies away, the new time rushes in. A bell that is only used for rituals works well, as do drums, rattles, and gongs.

A second way of creating sacred time is to start in darkness and then light candles. A third is to fill a cup or bowl and pass it for everyone to drink from. More than one of these ways can be used in one ritual, but use the same method or combination of methods each time. Pick one and stay with it; the whole point of doing it is to condition you and your family to shift into sacred time easily.

It is important also for there to be a distinct end to sacred time. The same sound that started the ritual can end it, or the candles can be blown out (something that children love to do), or the cup or bowl brought outside and poured out as an offering.

Wearing special clothing can make a time more special. It need not be the robes usually thought of as ritual garb. Remember the phrase "wearing your Sunday best?" Dressing up for the gods shows respect for them. Something special can be added to what you already wear. Romans covered their heads when they prayed. Greek priests sometimes wore headbands. A prayer shawl or a stole can be enough. Pendants work well, or other jewelry.

Colors can be used for different effects. For some rituals, particular color clothing is appropriate. Suggestions for these will be found with the rituals and in Appendix 3. Obvious choices are black for the dark of the moon, white for the full moon, and the green of newly growing things for May Day, but each occasion may have something appropriate.

Think about the body positions you take during the rituals. Associating one position with ritual makes for an easy transition to sacred time. One that is almost universal is stretching out your hands, palms up. Look at pictures of deities; they are often in the same position taken by their invokers.

The altar for these rituals is the family table, the kitchen or dining room table that is used every day or on special occasions. It is the place where the family gathers, where they eat, and where rituals will be performed, and as such it is sacred. The ancients knew this. For instance, Plutarch, in *Roman Questions* (p. 147, Question LXIV), tells us that the Romans never left the table empty and suggests that that is because it is a sacred place and sacred places should never be left empty. For this reason, it is good to leave something there (bread, candlesticks, flowers, a bowl of fruit), but it is more important to keep it clean and treat it with respect.

Several of the rituals call for the sprinkling of water. This sometimes serves to bless, with the drops of water carrying the blessing to whatever they touch, and other times it is a purification, a symbolic washing of the area. Dip your sprinkler into a bowl of water and shake it in the direction desired. A bundle of flowers or leaves can be used as a sprinkler. Flowers that are in season will add to the emphasis of a seasonal celebration. Other possible sprinklers include ribbons or threads tied to a stick, or a spoon-shaped tea infuser.

The sprinkling itself is something that will gladly be done by children. They may get overenthusiastic about it, but that is certainly no failing. A rattle can also be used to bless. Think of it as an aspergill, sprinkling blessing rather than water.

A form of ritual which has been neglected by Neo-Paganism but which is suitable for even the youngest children is prayer. All the types of prayer familiar from other religions can be used by Pagans, although the content and style will be different. I'll have more to say about this later. (See Chapter 6.)

Another frequently neglected ritual form is the giving of offerings. This formed a major part of both family and personal piety in pre-Christian days. It is prominent in the rituals in this book as well and will also be discussed in Chapter 6.

If you are a member of a coven or grove, family and group activities may conflict. There's only so much time, and you may find it necessary to celebrate with one of the two groups the day before or after a festival or moon observance. Which gets the official date is the question. You could opt for the family because your family is more important than your coven. (If it isn't, you need to reexamine your commitment to your family.) Or you could pick your coven on the grounds that psychic work is more affected by the date than celebrations are. Fortunately, many of the family seasonal rituals can be done in the daytime (some *should* be), while most covens or groves meet at night, but some of the other rituals may be a little trickier.

If you are the only one in your coven with a family, you could hold coven meetings at your home after the children have gone to bed. If there are other parents in the group, you could rotate. You could have a big sleepover with the group's children, assuming they will actually go to sleep early enough for you to do your work.

For many of the occasions, several rituals are given. Some are short and simple, while others are full-blown ceremony. The intent is to give a range of styles and complexity that can be tailored to fit your family, house, and taste. They should also show the range of rituals available to Pagans.

✧ 3 ✧

The Sacred Home

A home is a temple. This is true in almost all old traditions, and it should be especially true in Pagan families. As with other temples, it is a place where we encounter the sacred. It is worth remembering that a Pagan may make this encounter in the everyday world of home. This comes as no surprise; after all, a Pagan lives in the sacred at all times.

Guardians of the Threshold and Hearth

A home is more than a human construct. It is a living being, a microcosm. It is the world of those that live in it, and it has its spirits just as the world outside does. And just as the world has its God and Goddess, so the house has its threshold and hearth guardians. These two spots, together with the household shrine, are the most sacred spots in a house. Each has its guardian, and each has its rituals.

The threshold is the place where inside meets outside. It is the magic spot, the turning point. Such crossover spots are places of awesome power, and even when the threshold guardian may be worn down by familiarity he retains this power. What does it take to stand in between? Something may be learned from the most famous door-guardian, the Roman Janus. This god, who in pre-Hellenic days may have been one of the more important Roman deities, had two faces—he looked both ways. That is the sort of power required of such a guardian.

Doorside Shrine for Janus

The threshold guardian is the spirit who protects against external enemies. It is his job to invite good and avert evil. In short, this is your watchdog spirit. It is the house's god.

That is why it is customary to perform an act of respect on passing over the threshold: a reverent touch, a slight bow, a pause—anything to say to the spirit that you recognize and respect his presence.

Architecturally, the threshold is the doorsill. The threshold guardian, however, dwells in the doorposts and lintel as well. These are part of the passing from one place to another. The doorsill is treated as an altar, though, and it is on it that rites to the threshold spirit are held. The doorposts, however, are frequently the site of anointings and blessings, and figures of the threshold spirit may be found there, or next to them, either inside or out.

In days past, houses generally had only one door, but even when they had more the threshold spirit was held to inhabit only the main door, and his rites were only performed there. If you wish to recognize his presence at all of your doorways, there is nothing wrong with that, but it is not necessary. In an apartment building, the threshold to be honored is *yours*, not the building's.

If you envision your threshold guardian as Janus, he should be honored on January 1st, his feast day. However you envision him, a natural day on which to honor him is the anniversary of your moving into the house. Since threshold spirits are also the spirits of beginnings, they should be informed before any big changes are made in the life of the family.

The hearth is the heart and center of the home, the source of heat and life. This is not always true architecturally (although if it is a fireplace, that is the most efficient place for it to be), but it is always true spiritually. The threshold guardian may be the protector of the household, but in the hearth is the spirit of everything that is worth protecting. It protects not by repelling evil but by broadcasting good. It is the house's goddess.

Hearth guardians are usually female (male fire deities tend to be concerned with public fires). The best known are the Roman Vesta and the Greek Hestia, but the Celtic Brighid has a hearth fire function as well. Many cultures have chosen not to personify their hearth guardian, satisfied to acknowledge her presence without pretending to understand her nature. Indeed, even though the Romans named their hearth goddess, there was no statue in her temple in Rome.

If you wish to name your hearth guardian, but do not feel a closeness to either the Greco-Roman or Irish traditions, I recommend researching your ethnic heritage. Old forms of the word "fire" in ancestral languages can be used. For the oldest language of the ancestors of many of us, you can turn to Proto-Indo-European, and use "Purya." This is formed from the word for a household fire with a feminine ending added, and thus means "She Who is the Household Fire."

Our Hearth Guardian

Now you may be thinking that you don't have a hearth. Most of us don't have fireplaces; I don't, anyway. But you still have a hearth. In fact, you have more than one. Even if you don't have a fireplace you have a stove, and a furnace, and water heater—all of them hearths. If your stove is gas, you may even have a perpetual flame, your pilot light. Since the house can only have one center, the ritual location of the hearth goddess must be limited to one of these. The stove is best, as it is the place where food, the fuel of the body's fire, is prepared.

Put a candle or oil lamp next to your stove, to be lit when cooking your food, either daily or on special occasions. When you turn your stove or oven on, say:

> *I cook with* (your hearth guardian's name)*'s fire.*

This will keep her presence in your mind. It is also only polite to acknowledge such a deity frequently.

Household Guardians

The house has its spirits, but so does the household. Each family or household has a spirit or spirits to watch over it. This is an old concept in Paganism and is found virtually everywhere in the world.

These protective spirits come in many forms. Your family may have taken on a god or goddess with whom you feel especially close. That is certainly not to be discouraged. But the ones dealt with here are the homey spirits, the comfortable small ones that guide our everyday lives, and that are associated with only one family. Like hearth and threshold spirits, they are frequently nameless. If you choose to name yours, do not use the names of known deities. They are already responsible for more than one family. In Eastern Europe house spirits are referred to as "grandfather" or "grandmother," as a sign of respect for their wisdom and age. Any term which conveys the same to you can be used—Lord and Lady, Old Ones, etc.

Just who are these spirits, and where do they come from? There may be a family totem animal, perhaps taken from a coat of arms. There are ancestral spirits that have through time become associated with extended families, often with no explanation other than that they are traditional. There are spirits that guard over a particular house or part of it, and the barn, stove, and yard spirits of Eastern Europe. There are too many of these to give rituals for all of them or to discuss them in depth, but I will discuss several.

As an example to illustrate what these guardians are like, consider the Roman Lares. Originally agricultural spirits, they eventually became household guardians. They (there were always two) were shown as dancing youths, pouring out wine. They were frequently confused with the Penates, who protected the food supply. The Lares were offered incense, fruit, and wine. They were given the first serving at meals, and shared the family's lives. They stayed with the family wherever they moved, so they were spirits of the family, not of the physical house (which often had its own guardians). Here we have characteristics typical of household guardians—there is more than one, and they are concerned with food, offered to regularly, and have titles rather than names.

There is a strong connection between Household Guardians and the Ancestors. In many traditions they are one and the same, and the customs relating to them are similar in other traditions.

There are, technically, two types of ancestors in Paganism. There are the ancestors of all human beings, that lived in the primordial time when everything began. And there are our direct human ancestors that lived in the world just as we are living and are now gone. Neo-Paganism puts little emphasis on the first kind, however. This is probably because Neo-Pagans are not much interested in creation myths, having adopted the theories of science as explanations of origins.

The ancestors worked with by Neo-Pagans, then, are those who have lived among us and now are in the sacred realm. As such they are mediators between us and the spirit world, and also the obvious protectors of the family. They are still interested in us, with one foot in our world and one in the Otherworld. A belief in reincarnation does not mitigate their influence; the Otherworld is all times and all places, and reborn souls can therefore still be contacted through it.

Images of household guardians are kept in family shrines. (For more information on shrines see page 29.) Because of the namelessness of the guardians, the images need not be in human form. Possibilities include masks, a drum, generic male and/or female statues, or candles. For ancestral spirits the most common symbols, used in cultures as different as Rome and West Africa, are masks. Through them the ancestors look upon us, and if they are ones that can be worn, by doing so we take the ancestors' place.

Masks for images are easily made from papier-mâché. Blow up a balloon to head size. (If you don't intend to wear it, you can make a smaller mask.) A large bottle may also be used. Make a solution of wallpaper paste and water (follow the directions on the package) in a bowl. Tear strips of newspaper and dredge them through the paste. Put them on the balloon, crossing them in layers, until you have the thickness you want. Facial features can be built up from crumpled wads. If you want to wear the mask, it is easiest to make the eyeholes as you make it or to cut them before the mask is completely dry. If the mask is not going to be worn, eyeholes are not necessary. A form for the nose space can be made by folding a cardboard triangle in two and taping it to the balloon. Shape the paper strips over it. Dry the mask for a day or two. (On hot dry days the mask may take only a few hours to dry.) Then pop the balloon and dry the mask for a few more days. Once it is dry it can be painted. It will last longer if it is varnished. Masks can also be made in miniature.

To make the masks more easily recognizable as ancestor masks they can be painted with symbols of your ethnic background. It is very common for ancestor images to be white; that is the universal color for the dead, found in cultures of all races.

If you wish to use a drum for your guardian image, choose a flat one that can hang on the wall over your shrine. Decorate it with feathers, ribbons, stones, shells, or symbols painted on or burned into the wood. It can be used in family rituals, for shamanic healing, and just for fun. Its sound is the voice of the guardian.

Another good image is a god's eye. These can be made in pairs, male and female, by using different colors. Blue is traditional for male (the sky) and green for female (the earth). See Chapter 5 for directions on making them.

Like the Lares, guardian spirits frequently come in pairs, usually male and female, the mother and father of your family. For this reason you may want two symbols.

Images can be made or bought by the family, or they can be given as presents by parents of a couple getting married. Alternatively, the money or raw materials can be given as a present. If the materials the images are made from, or the images themselves, can come from the land one's ancestors came from, so much the better.

Even though they will later be founding their own nuclear families, children can still be given images of the household guardians when they move out. This will keep them under the protection of the family even though they may be living away from it. This is especially good for college or boarding school students, who are living separately from the family, but haven't fully left it.

Ritual for Calling a Household Guardian

You may already have a guardian spirit. Perhaps a particular object in your home has an air about it that says that it has become the dwelling place of a spirit. If you are this fortunate, work with the one you have. More likely, though, is that you will want to call one.

Gather together at your main dining table everyone who will be expected to be under the protection of the spirits, including animals if they can be brought indoors. If not, bring the images out to the animals at the end of the ritual to introduce them to the spirits. Wear ritual clothing if you wish, or your best clothing. One family member holds the images and another an offering of food and drink. In the shrine put an offering bowl with candles on either side and a rattle in front. Establish sacred time in your usual way. Meditate for a moment or two, synchronizing your breathing. (With small children this is simply a moment of silence.) While still breathing slowly, one adult says:

> *One heart beating*
> *One body breathing*
> *One life living*
> *calls guardian spirits to watch over us*
> *calls them out of the Great Unknown*
> *here to our home*
> *here to watch over us.*

If you wish to call an ancestral spirit, an adult then says:

> *Reaching out and reaching back*
> *to the time of our Ancestors*
> *we call to you:*
> *Here we are.*
> *The family goes on*
> *and joins with others*
> *in the weaving that makes the People.*

We did not spring out of nothing
We are neither the beginning nor the end
    of the chain.
You who have gone before
be happy for us.
You are here in our midst.
We do not live our lives separately from you.
We do not forget you.
See, we will keep your images in a place of honor:
in our shrine and in our hearts.
We will not forget you.
Do not forget us.
Watch over us.
Keep us safe.

Go to the shrine, light the candles, and put the guardian symbols there. They can be hung on the wall or supported by stands. God's eyes can be displayed by sticking them into bowls filled with sand or pebbles. An adult says:

The images of our ancestors
give form to their spirits
that they may watch over us
and help our daily lives.
What we offer to the images
is given to our ancestors.
They are part of us
and we are part of the chain of lives
from the beginning to the future.

Or, if it is not an ancestral spirit you are calling:

These images will serve as homes to our guardians,
a place for those who watch over us.
What we do in front of these,
we do in front of them.
What we give to these,
we give to them.
What we say to these,
we say to them.

(The "we ... to them" may be said by everyone.)

If you are using a drum, one of the adults holds it up and says:

This drum speaks with the voice of the Spirits,
the voice of those who watch over us.

Each family member then bangs on the drum at least once. It is then hung on the wall above the shrine.

After the images are installed, introduce all the family members to them. Then put the offering in the bowl, saying:

We do not only take.
We do not only ask.
We ourselves give.
We give ourselves.
We feed you, you feed us.
We watch over you, you watch over us.
Like strands in the same web, we are.

Shake the rattle at the images, turn, and shake it over the heads of each family member. Alternatively, a bowl of water can be drunk from by all present and then sprinkled on the images and the family.

One of the most common beliefs about household spirits is that having one is a responsibility. They don't just give, they must get too. In the Slavic traditions, for instance, guardian spirits who aren't given sufficient respect are known to bring bad luck on their families. Give offerings to them regularly. They seem to like cakes and milk best. (Leave the offerings overnight and the next day put them outside for animals or spirits of the wild.) Let them sit at your table at festivals. Tell them important events in your lives. Give them full respect.

There should be one day in the year when special attention is paid to them. If yours are ancestors they will be honored on Samhain. (See Chapter 7.) Other appropriate dates include the anniversaries of your wedding, engagement, moving, conception of the first child, moving in together; in short, a day that strikes you as being the beginning of your household. The Romans offered them cakes, milk, wine, and flowers monthly. If you choose to honor yours so well and so often I'm sure they will not complain.

The Household Shrine

Every house should have a spiritual center. In the old times the spiritual center and the geometric center was the same—the hearth. In the geometric center of the house it gave heat equally in all directions and served as a focus for home activities. If you are fortunate enough to have a fireplace, especially a central one, you have a ready-made spot for a household shrine.

The shrine can be many things, depending on your space available, creativity, and need for secrecy. If you don't have the obvious spot of a hearth, choose a place in the room you consider to be your home's spiritual center. The kitchen is a popular choice. That is where one of the fires of a modern home is, it is frequently where people gather to talk and work, it is where food is prepared and eaten, and it has counter space where a shrine can easily be established. Living rooms or family rooms are good choices, as are entrance ways (so the protective spirits can be revered going in and coming out). Find a spot where you won't be knocking things over but one that isn't pushed away in an inconspicuous corner.

The shrine contains an altar. This can be a table, a countertop, or a cabinet (enabling it to be closed if secrecy is required). It must be high enough to be used standing up and be in a place where it can be left set up all the time. If it is absolutely impossible to leave it set up, set it up and use it frequently, at least weekly.

In your shrine place images of your household guardians and of any of your family members' guardians or power animals. If you wish to use images of gods and goddesses but can't find any, remember that a rough statue made by you out of clay may actually be more powerful than something "perfect," and that many deities have animal or symbolic forms. Our shrine, for instance, contains a horse statue in honor of Rhiannon. Museum gift shops are good places to find both statues and photographs of statues of deities. Symbolic images can be used as well—a stone with a natural hole in it or a shell for the Goddess, and a pillar-shaped stone or an antler for the God. Put your sun and moon candles in the shrine as well. These large candles serve as representatives of the God and Goddess and are used in the solar and lunar rituals. (See Chapters 7 and 8.)

The biggest mistake most people make is cluttering a shrine up. They start collecting magical tools and images and end up with

Our Household Shrine

a shrine that looks like a rummage sale. Keep it simple. If there are particular deities that you relate to, go ahead and put their images there, but don't add every sacred object you can get your hands on.

This is not just a question of esthetics. A household shrine should be a place of peace and calm that can then radiate peace and calm to the whole house. If instead it is a jumble of dust collectors it will radiate disorder.

Think hard about the overall effect. Too many Pagans are pack rats. Their houses soon look as if they've raided every New Age bookstore and museum gift shop in the country. Unless you are a dyed in the wool Discordian, chaos is probably not what you're trying to convey.

You may find, however, that, regardless of clutter, something comes to you that wants to be put in your shrine. Perhaps a flea market will produce the perfect Goddess statue, but your shrine is already crowded. Then you have a decision to make. You can make another shrine in your home for the new piece. (If the piece appeals mainly to one family member, this is the best choice.) You can remove one of the pieces already in the shrine, giving it its own shrine. Perhaps something in the shrine has served its purpose in your family's life and can be given away. Perhaps the shrine can be rearranged to form several smaller shrines in the same area. Or perhaps you will simply decide to live with the clutter.

Whichever way you choose, this is not the time for one person's intuition to override the wishes of others. The family altar is a family concern, and decisions regarding it must be made as a family. Making the decision together is an act that will involve everyone in the religious life of the family and is therefore a religious act in itself.

In front of the images and candles put offering bowls. Here are placed the offerings to the household spirits when the ritual calls for it. They do not have to be left on the altar when they are not in use. Offerings are left overnight and then removed to outside. Fruit can be offered to the spirits and then eaten. They will take the spiritual part they need and thank you for the remembrance.

Use the shrine as often as possible. Your guardians can give advice and help if you take the time to honor them and ask for it. Whenever there is a crisis in your family life, your shrine should be the first place you go, to seek a moment of peace and reflection.

Family meetings should start with a visit to the shrine to ask the influence of the guardians on your discussions.

In the morning, before you start your day, take a moment of quiet in front of your shrine. The morning prayer I use is this:

> *Guardians of our household,*
> *I do you honor.*
> *Watch over us today as we go about our affairs.*
> *Keep us safe and happy and healthy.*

I also put my daughter's school lunches in front of the images and ask the guardians for blessings on them after I say this prayer.

Traditions to raid: Mezuzah (Jewish), Kamidana (Japanese).

Blessing a New Home

Right from the beginning of living in a new home you will want to have a proper relationship with it. You will want it to be sacred space, so that your living in it will be a sacred act.

Remember that moving into a new home means moving out of an old one. In the excitement of moving, don't forget to close off your ties to the home you're moving out of.

If your stay in your old home was pleasant you will want to bring as many influences with you as possible. Walk through it, the whole family together, and remember what has happened there. When you are finished with this, say:

> *We will hold these things in our hearts*
> *and they will always stay with us*
> *even as we go on to new places and ways.*
> *Spirits of this place,*
> *We invite you to come with us*
> *or, if you wish to stay,*
> *may there be peace between us always.*

When you are packing, leave your shrine until the last. As the soul of your home it needs to be there as long as it is your home. Make sure the movers know it is to be left alone. Before you pack it away, explain what is happening to your household guardians. They should have been told already, but you need to do it again as part of the leaving ritual. Bring the items in your shrine with you in a suitcase or box while you are actually traveling.

Of course, if you do not want to bring influences with you, you should do things differently. You might consider disposing of your shrine and establishing a completely new one at your new place. At the least, purify its objects the way you might purify new ones. Leave them outside in the sun or rain, or bury them in salt for a day or two. Dispose of the salt afterwards; don't use it for anything else. After purifying them, bless them again.

If there are objects that appear to be the center of bad influences, such as gifts from disruptive people or items in rooms where arguments were frequently held, abandon or purify them as well.

Ritual for Blessing a New Home

If you do this before moving in, so much the better, but it's never too late.

Blessing the Borders

If possible, go all around the outside of the home, censing and sprinkling as you go. If you do this, though, do not use salt or salt water. Salt can harm plants. If you wish to use all four elements, use sand or cornmeal for earth. Before you circle, say:

> *Blessed be this land.*
> *Our home stands on sacred space.*

As you go around it, pay attention to your land. You should know it already, but inspect it again with ritual awareness. If you can't go around the outside, go around the inside, keeping as close as possible to the walls.

If you live in an apartment or condominium that has common land, you can circle that. Without land, you will still need to make an imaginary trip around the borders of the building. Have everyone close their eyes while one of the adults describes the building's edges in as much detail as possible. Start at one corner and go clockwise around the building, giving approximate measurements.

If your children are too small to have a good grasp of feet or meters, give the measurements in terms of their or your body, or as steps. Include all architectural features—doors, windows, steps, pillars, fire escapes, etc.

If, on the other hand, you own some land (even just a yard), go around the entire border of it, paying special attention to its corners. You may want to put markers at them which you can use as altars for offerings to the spirits of the land. Stone markers are best because they are permanent, but posts will do. Posts have the advantage of being easy to carve, paint, or burn a face or protective symbols in if you wish. (See Appendix 1 for protective symbols.) These can be naturally shaped stones, but pillars are better because their impression of verticality clashes with the horizontal ground and says, "Here is a border." As phallic symbols, they also serve as reminders of the power of the border spirits.

Border markers needn't be large. A foot high is fine. The important thing is that they be visible, at least to those who know their significance. This shouldn't be a problem if the land is your own, but on common land you may need to go without, or you can use sticks pushed in flush with the ground, small rocks, or features already in place. Sometimes when a house is built, concrete markers are placed at the corners of the property by the builders. Look for them, and use them if they are already there.

Before you erect each marker, pour out some wine and place an egg and grain or cakes in the hole where it will be put. As you do so, say:

> *We give these gifts to the spirits of the land*
> *who were here before we were.*
> *Though we may now claim this land as ours*
> *it was yours long before*
> *and it will be yours when we are gone.*
> *Do not begrudge us its use*
> *but may there be friendship between yours and ours.*

Then erect the marker while saying:

> *God of the borders, watch over our land.*

Both the spirits of the land and the god of the borders should be given offerings on special occasions such as the anniversary of moving to the house or when your household is in need of particular protection.

In some parts of the British Isles the borders were honored in the past by entire villages in a custom called "Beating the Bounds." The villagers would process around the village's borders, and at landmarks or corners where children were whipped or ducked in cold water. The explanation given was that it would "help them remember." Similar rituals were held in Greece, Rome, Russia, Norway, and other parts of Europe. I'm not suggesting you whip your children, but they could be the ones to put out the offerings.

Border guardians rarely have names, but the Romans called theirs Terminus. He will not mind if you call him that as well.

Threshold Blessing

Bless the main threshold before entering for the rest of the ritual. If you wish to bless the others as well, do so, but without the invocation of the threshold guardian. Bless the threshold with the elements and leave a small offering beside it, saying:

> *Watcher of the threshold*
> *Who looks both ways*
> *Who guards coming in*
> *Who guards going out*
> *Watch over our family*
> *and all of our guests.*
> *Guard our coming in*
> *Guard our going out.*
> *Open onto a home filled with love and peace*
> *and hospitality for all guests.*

If this is your first home, add:

> *God of all beginnings,*
> *look with special favor on this,*
> *our first home.*

If you have an image of a threshold guardian, install it near the main door.

Cleansing

It is an unfortunate fact that many of the things that have happened in your new home before you move in might not have been pleasant. Unpleasant happenings leave their traces behind and could cause problems if allowed to stay. The first thing that should be done after entering, then, is to clean. An actual physical cleaning is a good idea, especially vacuuming and sweeping, both wonderful ways to banish. If you concentrate on banishing undesired influences while you clean, it will be especially effective.

After the cleaning, use all your noisemakers, bells, rattles, drums, and horns. If you have a drum for your household guardian, definitely use it. Ritually, noise is said to disturb harmful spirits. Psychologically, it acts as a catharsis, and the following silence seems peaceful in comparison. (And children will love it.) Make as much noise as possible while shouting:

> *Everything that is bad*
> *Everything that could hurt*
> *Go away,*
> *Get out!*

Repeat the last two lines as many times as you feel necessary.

Blessing the Hearth

If you have a fireplace, light a small fire in it, saying:

> *The heart of our home is burning brightly.*

Give it offerings, especially of incense, saying:

> *Queen of the hearth, be here in our home.*
> *Warm it and light it.*
> *Keep love's flames high.*

If you use a Brighid's cross (see the Imbolc rite, Chapter 7), hang it over the mantle. Then use a taper to carry a flame from the fire to any pilot lights you might have. By doing this, all the flames in your house become one flame, the flame of your hearth guardian.

If you don't have a fireplace, perform this rite by your stove, lighting the pilot light if there is one, or a candle or oil lamp next to the stove if there isn't. Leave this burning throughout the ritual.

The Shrine

Set up your household shrine. Leave offerings of bread and salt. If you are establishing a new household after starting a new family, you will have to perform the ritual to attract a household guardian.

Consecration by the Elements

On the altar of your shrine put unlit incense (air), a lit candle (fire), a bowl of water (water), a plate of salt (earth), and a flower, crystal, or mirror (spirit). Raise the image of each element up in turn and turn clockwise around to present it to the house. One of the adults says:

> We bless this house by air
> the breaths of song
> of talking with friends,
> the slow breaths of meditation and prayer
> and the quiet breaths of sleep.
> By air be clean
> Be fresh
> Be pure.

> We bless this house by fire
> The fire that will warm it
> The fire that will cook our food
> The fire that burns within us
> The fire of life and love
> By fire be clean
> Be fresh
> Be pure.

> We bless this house by water
> in all its many forms
> All that we will drink
> All that we will cook with
> All that we will clean ourselves with
> By the very blood that runs through our veins
> By water be clean
> Be fresh
> Be pure.

We bless this house by earth
from which it springs, on which it rests
We are creatures of earth
Living upon it
Living from it
Living within it
By earth be clean
Be fresh
Be pure.

We bless this house by spirit
by active and passive we bless it
The spirit that sustains us
wrapping around us
keeping us safe in its arms
By spirit be clean
Be fresh
Be pure.

Children can do the presenting, and older children can say the words. "Be clean, be fresh, be pure" can be said by everyone.

Mix the salt with the water and light the incense from the candle. You now have consecrated water which combines the two female elements (earth and water) and burning incense which combines the two male elements (air and fire). Use these to bless the house, sprinkling and censing as you go. The sprinkling can be done by quite young children, and the censing by slightly older ones.

Sealing the Windows and Doors

Go to each window, door, or other opening (chimney, dryer vent, etc.). This can be done as you come to them while you are censing and sprinkling. With an athame, wand, or your hand, draw a symbol of protection over it. (See Appendix.) Say:

This opening is sealed,
guarded against all that would harm.

Blessing of Rooms

Bless each room as you come to it by sprinkling, censing, and saying a blessing. Suit the blessing to the room and the function it will perform. For example:

*May this kitchen be blessed
that all the food prepared in it
will give not only nourishment
but pleasure.*

*May this bathroom be blessed,
a place of cleaning and health,
that all who use it may be refreshed.*

*May this bedroom be blessed,
so that it might give rest and peace
to all who sleep in it.*

*May this guest room be blessed.
May it help us to fulfill our duties as hosts
and bring blessings to our guests.*

*May this living room be blessed
that it may be a place of fun and relaxation
for all who use it.*

*May this storage room be blessed
that it may keep in safety
the goods that are entrusted to it.*

Offerings to Outstanding Natural Features

Go outside and tour your yard. Pay special attention to any outstanding natural features—large rocks, streams, small hills, etc. Say hello to each tree and leave a small offering of food and drink. If there are too many to do this individually, do it at each group.

The Meal

Come inside and have a meal. Use your best place settings, and one of the meal prayers (Chapter 6). The food should include bread (so you may never hunger) and salt (that your life might always have flavor). These really should be given to you by someone welcoming you to the neighborhood, but you'll probably have to improvise. Don't forget to provide them for others, though. You can explain it as an old custom (which it is). It is most common in Eastern Europe, but the combination of bread and salt is found in many cultures, among the Romans and the Irish, for instance. Many Americans are familiar with it from Frank Capra's *It's a Wonderful Life*.

As soon as possible after the house blessing, have a house-warming party. One of the responsibilities of a householder is hospitality. It is also one of the joys.

Traditions to raid: Terminalia (Roman; February 23rd), Beating the Bounds (British; dates vary).

4

Celebrations of Birth

Children are born religiously pure. No matter what this little soul's karma, in this incarnation she is without flaw. No one is responsible for another's actions, so this condition will continue until she is old enough to make her own mistakes. It was this attitude that allowed Lakota children to wander unchecked through sacred ceremonies—the sacred cannot be disturbed by the sacred.

The point of rituals performed for babies is not to purify the child but to incorporate her into the family and the community, and extend the protection of the gods and household guardians over her.

Welcoming

As soon as the baby is seen, whether born or adopted, say:

Little One, welcome to our family.
We have waited so long to see your face
and sing to you our welcoming songs.

All members of the family should do this, including other children who are old enough. Children too young to say the words may give a hug instead.

After the birth it is appropriate for the mother to make a special offering or prayer of thanksgiving to the birth goddess to whom she has prayed for help. Suitable offerings include bread, cookies, eggs, milk, breast milk, flowers, and sandalwood, rose, or mint incense. When offering, this prayer can be used:

> *Mother of All,*
> *We have been pregnant together*
> *and now I, like you, have given birth.*
> *Thank you for bringing me through this time*
> *and for helping me to deliver a beautiful child.*

Blessing

Many people saw how in the mini-series *Roots* a father presented his newborn to the earth and sky. This delightful custom is widespread, appearing not only in Africa but among Indo-Europeans and the Japanese. Its meaning is clear: the child belongs to earth and sky, and she is being brought before them for their acknowledgement and blessing. As soon as the mother feels up to it, take the baby outdoors. The mother places the baby on the ground and says:

> *Born of woman*
> *Born of earth.*
> *The Mother knows Her children.*

The father picks up the child, holds her up to the sky, and says:

> *Conceived by man*
> *Conceived under the sky.*
> *The Father knows His children.*

One or both of them will then say:

> *You are the child of earth and sky*
> *and you live your life between them,*

Mother and Father to you
and to all living things.

Some people plant a tree at the time of birth. If you can be relatively sure to be at the same place when the child is grown up, this is a lovely custom. Be careful, though; the fate of your child may be bound with that of the tree. If you wish to dispose of the afterbirth or umbilical cord ritually, it may be buried with the planting of the tree. This will tie the child to the place even more.

Presentation to Household Guardians

Although it may be assumed that the spirits of the household, like the parents themselves, have learned to know and love the child during the pregnancy, she must still be presented to them. This inaugurates her ritual relationship with them.

Place the baby on the threshold and say:

> *Guardian of the threshold,*
> *Here is one of us.*
> *A new member of our family has come home.*
> *Remember her.*
> *Watch over her comings in.*
> *Watch over her goings out.*

Touch a cup of water, milk, or wine to her lips, and sprinkle some of it on the threshold. Take the baby to the household shrine and say:

> *Guardians of our household,*
> *Here is one of us.*
> *A new member of our family has come home.*
> *Remember her.*
> *Watch over her as she goes about her daily affairs.*
> *Keep her safe.*
> *Keep her happy.*
> *Keep her healthy.*

Again touch the cup to her lips and offer some to the guardians. Then place the cup in front of the guardian images and leave it overnight. In the morning, offer the rest to the spirits of the wild.

Naming and Dedication

Although the child may have been introduced to earth and sky and presented to the household guardians, there is still one more ritual that should be performed, when the baby is officially given her name. Having taken her place in the family, she is now presented to the larger community. Since a name is what a baby is called by others, and since relatives may well expect a celebration, this is best done with your extended family and friends.

This ritual is commonly called "saining" by Neo-Pagans. The name derives from a northern dialect of English, and is simply that dialect's version of "signing." The reference is to making the sign of the cross over the child, and thus was a term for baptism. Some Pagans may wish to avoid it on these grounds, while others may think that since it is no longer used by most English-speakers in its original meaning they need have no more hesitation using it than Christians have using the originally Pagan "Easter" for their most holy day.

Naming should take place after the baby's umbilical cord drops off. Until then the baby is still connected spiritually to her mother in a way that she is not to others.

There is no uniquely Pagan way to choose a name for your child. Some Pagan cultures have chosen names that refer to events surrounding children's conceptions or births. Others have practiced divination. Still others have used family names, names that reflected the order or day of birth, or simply names the parents liked.

Many of the usual names found in our culture are fine. Many Pagans like to name their children after Pagan heroes or gods. This is fine, although it might be best to avoid the names of the highest gods. Ancient Pagans that included gods in their names used such compounds as "Mithra's friend," or "Servant of Lugh." Using unmodified gods' names for children has generally been a sign that the gods are no longer believed in. Children can also be named after ancestors, especially boys after their fathers' people and girls after their mothers'. If possible names have been pared down to a small number without an obvious choice, one can be chosen through divination. This can be done simply by writing the names on pieces of paper or tiles and then drawing one blindly from a bowl. Before doing this, pray:

> *Lady and Lord,*
> *Divine Parents,*
> *You have given us a child.*
> *Now help us choose a name.*

If you don't know the sex of the child yet, you'll have to do this twice, of course.

The main purpose of a dedication is to name the child. Its secondary purpose is to place the child under the protection of the deities. This is a natural desire. Childhood is almost universally seen as a dangerous time and children need all the help they can get. It is also natural to want your children to grow up with the same world view and morals. Children need guidance in this and what other spiritual path is a parent more qualified to teach than the one he is on?

To help the parents in this task, and to ensure that the child is seen as the responsibility of the community, the ritual appoints godparents. They are called "guardians" in the ritual to avoid confusion with Christian baptism, but that is perhaps an awkward term. Although honorable enough, it may be confused with the concept of legal guardian. If you wish to use "guardian," though, "godparent" might be just the word to use when explaining the position to non-Pagans.

The ritual is written to be done by more than just the immediate family. If at all possible, that is how it should be performed. The child is being welcomed into the world, and the world is not just the family. It may therefore be performed in the presence of understanding non-Pagans. Please brief them beforehand. Inviting them to a "baptism" that turns out to be Pagan rather than Christian would not be a good introduction to Paganism.

As well as the guardians, this ritual calls for representatives of the elements. Older children may serve in this role.

The ritual may be impossible to perform as written since not all Pagans know other Pagans who can take part. It can even be done by the parents alone. My wife and I did it that way ourselves, when we were living in England, thousands of miles away from our families and friends. Remove the challenges to the parents and guardians and the passing of the baby around the people. The parents then take the roles of the Priest, Priestess, and representatives of the elements. Instead of one presiding officer they should share the words.

The declarations of what it means to be a parent or a guardian are based on my own understanding of those responsibilities. If your understanding is different, then rewrite these to reflect it. Since these are essentially oaths, they should be written beforehand rather than made up on the spot. The parents and guardians are binding themselves to the child and to their responsibilities towards her. They are not expressing themselves here; they are expressing their willingness to step into the roles that have existed since sexual reproduction has.

Ritual

Because this ritual is attended by people who are not in the immediate family, it will usually be held outside the home. You will need to create sacred space, then, by casting a circle. Put a table in the middle of the circle and put on it whatever you will need for the circle casting, water, consecrated oil, and milk. The representatives of the elements go to their respective directions, holding symbols of their elements. Create your sacred space as usual. If you like, when you call the directions you can say:

> *Spirits of the East*
> *Spirits of Air*
> *A new child has been born to us.*
> *Come to see her.*
> *Come to bless her.*
> *Come to us who wait for you.*
>
> *Spirits of the South*
> *Spirits of Fire*
> *A new child has been born to us.*
> *Come to see her.*

Come to bless her.
Come to us who wait for you.

Spirits of the West
Spirits of Water
A new child has been born to us.
Come to see her.
Come to bless her.
Come to us who wait for you.

Spirits of the North
Spirits of Earth
A new child has been born to us.
Come to see her.
Come to bless her.
Come to us who wait for you.

Call the Goddess in a Mother form—Diana, Rhiannon, Demeter, Isis, etc. Call the God as All-Father—Cernunnos, Woden, Zeus, Dagda, etc. For instance, you can say:

Diana, Our Mother
We ask your presence here
to bless this child we bring before you.

If the child is a girl, the Priest presides, and if the child is a boy, the Priestess does. (The form given is for a girl.)
The Priest says:

We meet today to bless this child, to place her on
the path to happiness, and to name her. Naming is
no slight thing, for it is said that the name is the
thing. The path is no slight thing, for of the many
that she will find, perhaps there is only one path
that will lead her to happiness. And let no one dis-
parage the blessing of the gods, the protection of the
elements, and the love of the People.

You who come before us, who are you?

The parents answer:

(Their names), *parents of this child.*

He says:

> *Do you know what it is to be a parent?*

They reply:

> *It is to love and nurture,*
> *to watch a child grow*
> *and lead her to the path to right living*
> *that she may know the good*
> *and, knowing it, choose it.*
> *It is to teach and to learn.*
> *It is a way of great joy and great pain.*
> *It is to take in and cherish so that one day*
> *   you might let go.*
> *It is the greatest responsibility we can take:*
> *For our love has become manifest in a person*
> *and who may know its end?*

He says:

> *You answer well. May the Goddess and God,*
> *whose love gives birth to the world,*
> *guide you in your responsibilities.*

The Priestess then challenges the child's guardians, saying:

> *You who stand here with these parents,*
> *   who are you?*

They answer:

> (Their names), *chosen to be guardians*
> *   for this child.*

She asks:

> *Do you know what it is to be a guardian?*

They answer:

> *It is to open the many paths before a child,*
> *to show her the ways she may take,*
> *to help her choose that which is hers,*
> *and, once she is on it, to help her live by it.*
> *It is to be second parents,*
> *ready to counsel, ready to love,*
> *always to be there when needed.*

She says:

> *You answer well. May the Goddess and the God,*
> *whose love gives birth to the world,*
> *guide you in your responsibilities.*

The parents place the baby on the altar, where the presiding officer traces a pentagram on her forehead with water, saying:

> *Lord and Lady, keep this child pure.*
> *Let all that is wrong be far from her.*

The parents then take the child to the east, where a representative of the Spirit of Air blesses her by censing, blowing, waving a fan, or ringing a bell, and says:

> *Little one, receive the blessing of Air.*
> *Keep, as long as you can, your holy innocence.*
> *Greet each day joyously,*
> *Always rejoicing in its newness.*
> *Greetings from the Spirit of Air,*
> *Your protector and friend.*

The parents then go clockwise to the other quarters. At the south the baby is passed over the candle flame (be careful of long garments), while the representative of the Spirit of Fire says:

> *Little one, receive the blessing of Fire.*
> *Receive the creative spark to dream with,*
> *the courage to keep your ideals,*
> *and the will to make your dreams come true.*

> *Greetings from the Spirit of Fire,*
> *Your protector and friend.*

At the west, the baby is sprinkled with water, while the representative of the Spirit of Water says:

> *Little one, receive the blessing of Water,*
> *the womb from which we all come.*
> *Yield gracefully to what must be,*
> *knowing the treasures you hold within.*
> *Greetings from the Spirit of Water,*
> *Your protector and friend.*

At the north, the baby is sprinkled with salt, sand, or corn-meal, while the representative of the Spirit of Earth says:

> *Little one, receive the blessing of Earth,*
> *the earth from which you grew.*
> *Be strong in silence and fertile in growth.*
> *The North is darkness, out of which comes light.*
> *Greetings from the Spirit of Earth,*
> *Your protector and friend.*

The baby is then laid on the ground in the center of the circle. If the ground is too cold, touch her foot to dirt in a bowl. While this is done, the Priestess says:

> *Receive the blessings of our Mother Earth:*
> *May She protect you all of your days,*
> *wrapping Her arms around you*
>   *as you go your way.*

The Priest holds her up to the sky and says:

> *Receive the blessings of our Father Sky:*
> *May He protect you all of your days,*
> *watching over you as you go your way.*

The parents then hold the child in the center of the circle, while the presiding officer traces a pentagram over her, saying:

Little one, receive the blessings of Spirit,
which binds the four together,
from which they are formed,
and through which they are made manifest.
The Spirit is your home;
Be open to it, both gentle and vigorous:
Return to the center in times of trouble.

The parents carry the baby to the altar, where the presiding officer puts a drop of milk in her mouth, saying:

May you always have plenty.

He puts a drop of wine in her mouth, saying:

May you always be happy.

He puts a drop of water in her mouth, saying:

May you always be pure.

The Priestess then traces a pentagram with oil on the baby's breast, saying:

Little one, you are (her name),
This will be your name until the time comes
when you are admitted to full worship
*   before the gods.*
Bear it well, and may it do you honor.

The Priest stretches out his hands over the baby and says:

May the Lady and the Lord
smile gently upon you.
May you choose your path wisely
and walk it well.
May you be gentle and strong.
May you be loving and wise.
And may you be happy
For the world is good.

The parents take her to the four quarters, saying:

> *Spirit of the* (direction), *behold* (her name)
> *Welcome her to this world.*

The baby will then be passed among the people present. Each will kiss her and say:

> *Welcome,* (her name)*:*
> *Much love to you.*

It is also traditional for each person present to give a blessing or expression of best wishes.

When the baby reaches the guardians, they say:

> *Welcome,* (her name)*:*
> *May you love as you will always be loved.*

The parents say the same when the child is returned to them.

When farewells are said to the Goddess and the God at the end of the ritual, the Priestess says:

> *Mother and Father,*
> *we thank you.*
> *For the gift of life*
> *and the beauty of the world in which to live it.*
> *For the gift of love*
> *and the wonderful people with which to share it.*
> *But most of all today for* (her name),
> *who is both life and love.*
> *We ask your blessings as you depart.*
> *Hail and farewell.*

When she dismisses the Spirits of the directions, she says:

> *Spirit of the* (direction),
> *We thank you for your help.*
> *Go now in peace, but be never far away*
> *and answer quickly when* (her name) *calls for you*
> *that you might aid her in her need.*

Birthdays

In American culture birthdays are already traditional occasions. There is a song, food, candle-lighting, gift-giving, and wish-making—all the earmarks of a folk festival. Pagans wouldn't wish to take anything away.

But more could be added. Most families, in fact, have extra traditions. Some of these are passed on through the family, some are ethnic, and some are made up on the spot. Some you do once and discover the next year that the child considers them traditions.

When the child gets up in the morning of his birthday, he should wash, dress in special clothes, and then go or be taken to the family shrine. There he makes an offering. If he has his own protective spirit its image should have been placed there or he can place it there himself. If not, the offering will be to the family deities and guardians. Indeed, even with a personal spirit, these added offerings are desirable. You will need one candle in front, or one on either side of the image. If the child is old enough, he lights it; if not, one of the parents does. Then the offerings are given with a short prayer. Here are some examples:

> *The wheel has turned again*
> *since I came into this world.*
> *I thank the God and Goddess.*
> *I thank the Watchers of my house.*
> *I thank the Spirits of the Earth.*
> *Thank you for everything you have done for me*
> *   in this year.*
> *Be with me in my new year*
> *and I will remember you.*

> *Ancestors*
> *Old Ones*
> *You who have lived before me:*
> *I am here to show you that I have not*
> *   forgotten you.*
> *Thank you for helping me to grow*
> *   through the year.*
> *Help me to grow through the year to come.*

> *Mother of Everything*
> *Father of Everything*
> *Thank you for everything.*
> *Here are some gifts for you*
> *for all you have done.*

If the child is old enough, he can compose his own prayers. They don't have to be the same each year, of course.

The offerings can be incense, food, drink, or flowers. After the birthday, take whatever offerings are left out to your yard or to a wild place and leave them there.

One of the meals during the day should be with just the immediate family present. Put the household guardian images on the table, with the image of the child's personal guardian, if he has one. At the end of the meal, the parents say:

> *The year has turned ( ) times since you were born*
> *and now it has turned again.*
> *The God and the Goddess have watched you grow*
> *and will stay with you as this next year turns.*

Then they each bless the child. This is a personal blessing and they should write their own for the occasion. An example of a short one would be:

> *May the Lord and Lady bless you*
> *and watch and guard you*
> *as you grow through the year to come.*

The party follows this. This is the time for giving presents from the family.

❦ 5 ❧

Teaching Children

Much of the way in which Pagans want their children to grow is not uniquely Pagan. We want children who are honest, responsible, helpful, intelligent, loving, and happy. Who doesn't? These are the common values of our culture.

Paganism's unique contribution to values is its attitude toward nature. Helpful, yes, but not just to humans. Intelligent, yes, but not at the expense of the planet. Much of Pagan child rearing, then, is geared toward developing a love of the world. Less emphasis is placed on those things that seem specifically religious—belief systems and practices. Those are important too, and our children must be taught them, but without the right attitude toward the world they are useless and perhaps even harmful.

Pagan instruction isn't a one-shot thing—this is what we believe and do, now run along. Nor is it even a set course—fulfill these lesson requirements and we'll be all set. At its best, the teaching goes on all the time. You compost, you turn off lights when you're not using them, you work in the garden. And you make sure your child is doing these things along with you.

Remember that Paganism is a religion of doing. Much of your teaching will take place when you are performing the rituals in the rest of this book. At the very least you will have to explain why they are done. (Children are very good at asking why.)

Children learn best by parental example, second best by discovering through doing, and third best by active teaching. Parental example requires constant awareness of what is being done by the parent and why. The more fully you live a Pagan life, the more your child will learn about Paganism, and the more she will want to live a Pagan life as well. Beyond that, not much can be said except "be fair." Fairness is the first ethical concept children learn. Indeed, if there is any inborn root to ethics it must surely be fairness.

Teaching through doing involves many things. Rituals are important teaching tools. They show what a Pagan does. Many other activities provide useful teaching.

When choosing activities for young children it is important to remember that you are not training priests or priestesses. You are working with children, trying to awaken them spiritually and give them a framework in which to do it. It is best, therefore, to hold back on the mind-blowing, life-transforming experiences as well as on psychic exercises. These can be reserved for adolescence, a time of natural life-transformation and awakening powers.

Activities

Meditation

There are many forms of meditation, from the quiet empty sitting of zazen to the more active forms involving chanting or dance. The very quiet forms can be hard for young children. Still, it is good training for them; it might even teach them how to sit still for a while and the concentration it develops will help them in other things. Try doing it for short periods, two minutes for instance. If they react poorly, back off for a while. Let them see you do it, and make sure they know that they can meditate too when they are old enough.

Don't be discouraged if your children are uncooperative. My daughter hated meditating, so we stopped. Then I discovered, some time later, that she had been doing it on her own. Plant the seed and let it grow.

To meditate, sit with your back straight, your body relaxed, and your hands in your lap. Try to sit in the lotus position. Children are very flexible and very proud of their ability to sit in unusual positions. This is especially true if you have troubles doing that yourself. Breathe slowly and evenly, being sure to push from your diaphragm. Count your breaths, counting either on the inhale, exhale, or both. Count to five and then start over.

Chanting and Singing

Children love to sing, and so do Pagans. See the reference section for a list of some recordings of Pagan songs. Pagan periodicals usually have advertisements for these.

Self-Blessings

These give the child a short ritual that he can do on his own. A number of these have been published. A very simple one can be done with a bowl of water. The child holds his hands over it and says:

> *May this water be blessed*
> *with the power of the Goddess*
> *and the power of the God*
> *so it will bless me.*

He then anoints himself. The places blessed can vary, but usually the forehead is included. If he is preparing for work or sports, he may wish to anoint the parts of his body used in those activities. Self-blessings may also be used for morning or evening prayers.

Mask Making

Masks have long been used by Pagans. They have been used to change shamans into their power animals, to invoke gods and ancestors into their worshipers, and to transform actors in sacred drama into the deities they play. Masks overlap the border between fantasy and reality as well as that between magic and fun. They can give power, teach a child to identify with an animal or spirit, free a child from normal constraints, and just be fun. With a mask a child can be something different, trying on a new way of being for size.

The easiest material to make masks from is paper. Easy temporary ones can be made from paper bags or cardboard. A paper plate can be turned into a mask by cutting eye and mouth holes and punching a hole on each side for strings or elastic to hold it on. Faces and designs can then be drawn on with crayons, markers, or paint. Feathers, ribbons, and seeds can be glued on. Other items such as large feathers and seashells can be attached with ribbon. More permanent masks can be made with papier mâché. (See Chapter 3.)

God's Eyes

These are designs made from two sticks and colored yarn. (See Figure 1.) Made in elemental colors they can edge a magic circle. Made large in the color of spirit, with smaller crosslets at the ends of the sticks in the elemental colors, they can be an educational protective wall hanging. They can sit in the family shrine as symbols of the household guardians. Yellow ones make good solar decorations, especially if made with six or eight arms.

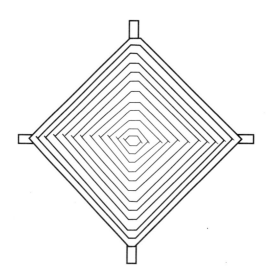

Figure 1. God's Eye

Take two or more sticks or dowels and cross them in the middle. Take a piece of yarn and tie the sticks together in a cross shape. Wrap the yarn around one stick, looping it over. Wrap it around the next stick, looping it under this time. Keep doing this, alternating the direction of looping, until you run out of yarn or sticks, or until the god's eye is big enough. Leaving a portion of the sticks protruding from the yarn when it is done will prevent the last loops from slipping off. Tie the last bit off and cut the yarn flush with the knot. Colors can be changed, either mixing different colors or using two or more shades of one color.

Shrine

Have each child make a shrine in his room. This should be a shrine, not an altar. In other words, it should have a deity figure as a focus and be for devotion rather than magical work. Go through some simple self-blessing and worship rituals with him. Then leave him to it. Tell him to perform some ritual at the shrine at least once a day (first thing in the morning or last thing at night) for a month.

How complicated the shrine is will depend on the age of the child. Very young children may be content with a statue or drawing and a bowl for offerings. Older children can use candles and incense, once they are taught how to use them safely. The rituals performed at it will also vary. For young children you will most likely need to write a short prayer or two that they can use. Older children can write their own or wait for the deity to inspire one in them.

Rattle Making

Rattles can be made from many substances. The most traditional is a gourd. Choose one with no blemishes. Some gourds can be used simply dried, with the seeds to make the sounds. Usually, though, they need help. Cut off the gourd's end and scrape out as much as you can. Keep it in a dry warm place until dry. If too much flesh is left behind or if the gourd is not dried carefully, it will become moldy. When the gourd is dry, put some of the seeds back in, along with some pebbles, and plug the end.

Papier mâché is easier, especially when working with children. Blow up a balloon to the desired size and cover it with strips of paper soaked in wallpaper paste. Put on several layers for strength, alternating the direction the strips are laid. Leave a thin spot at the top and an open spot at the bottom for the stick. When the rattle is dry remove the balloon. (It will probably have collapsed already; if not, just pop it.) Put noise makers inside. It is traditional to include both quartz pebbles and seeds. Popcorn works fine for seeds. Shape a stick to fit the hole in the bottom. Carve the top of the stick so that it is thinner than the rest. After filling the rattle with the noise makers, put the stick through the bottom hole. Where it touches the top, make a hole just large enough for the stick to come out. Seal the two holes, top and bottom, with more strips of paper. When it is completely dry, decorate it with paint, feathers, or ribbons.

Easier still is to take a small plastic bottle such as an empty vitamin bottle and fill it with pebbles and seeds. Put the top back on, and you have an instant rattle.

Image Making

Make images for the child's shrine or make the ones for the household shrine with the child. You can use clay or papier mâché for statues, or they can be drawn or painted on paper, cardboard, or wood. Clay that can be fired in a regular oven is available in art supply stores. Seeds, sticks, or stones can be used to make collages for images.

Nature Journal

With your child, keep track of one year, noting dates of flowering, appearance of leaves, changing and dropping of leaves, migrations of birds, behavior of animals, weather, etc.

Observing a Space

Choose an area about one yard square and mark it off. On your own land this can be done with rope. On public land it can delineated by natural features or marked with sticks pushed flush into the ground. Observe it daily for one hour for a short period (two weeks, for instance) and then weekly for longer (several months to a year). Call on the spirits of the place each time. Do not interfere with it, observe it only.

Garden

Have your child choose the plants, plant, care for, harvest, and prepare the garden for winter. The size and complexity can increase with age. Have your child write and carry out a garden blessing. Remember that a garden can be a window box, plants in pots on a balcony, or even an indoor herb garden kept by a sunny window.

Mythical Character Costume Party

Invite your child's friends to come to a party dressed as mythical characters. You may have to limit this to Pagan children.

Drumming

Drumming is the best thing that ever happened to Neo-Paganism, and the earlier a child gets involved the better. Drums can be used for communication, ecstasy induction, direction, dance rhythm, or just plain fun. Drum with your child, either just with your drum or keeping a beat to recorded music. Once she can keep a simple beat she should be encouraged to bring her drum to a Pagan gathering. There will probably be rituals where she can drum. The experience of being part of a group of drummers contributing to a ritual is overpowering. Children have few opportunities to take part in rituals in such an active way.

Inexpensive drums are available in music and toy stores. Small frame drums costing less than thirty dollars can be ordered through most instrument stores. For an even less expensive drum, a shoe box, oatmeal box, or plastic container works well.

Storytelling

Stories can be myths, fairy tales, or made up on the spot. They can be told by the parent to the child or the child to the parent. One can start it and then hand it off to another who must then continue it for a while before again passing it on. The traditional time for storytelling is winter, when there is little to do outside and it is comfortable to settle around a fire and talk. Hearing the old stories is one of the most important things that can happen in a Pagan child's life. The stories are a link with the Pagans of old times as well as models for ritual and life.

When telling stories use all your abilities. Use props and voices, and don't be afraid to embroider the tales, provided the essentials are kept.

Decorations

Decorations for celebrations can be made with children. One easy way to make them is to roll oven-firing clay thinly (between 1/8 and 1/4 inch) and then use cookie cutters or kitchen knives to cut suitable shapes—moons, suns, seasonal symbols, and such. These shapes can be decorated with designs scratched into them before they dry or they can be painted after firing.

Non-Pagan Activities

There are many activities sponsored by non-Pagans that can be part of a Pagan education. Summer camps, nature and science centers, and scouting all teach knowledge of and respect for nature. Art museums sometimes give workshops in skills such as mask making. Community centers and ethnic societies give lessons in traditional dance and music.

Class

Although the most important part of your child's religious education will take place in informal or ritual contexts, more formal schooling can be integrated into a Pagan education program. Formal schooling is one of the ways our culture says that something is important. If a child's Christian friends are off to Sunday school or CCD and her Jewish friends are off to Hebrew school but the child never has Pagan school she may begin to wonder just how important Paganism can be. And she may simply feel left out. Slipping in Paganism when it comes up may result in not teaching it at all; sometimes things just don't come up when we want them to.

The more formal aspects of Paganism can be presented in a weekly class. It should last no more than an hour. Treat it as importantly as any other appointment. This will show your child how important Paganism is. Weeks you celebrate special occasions you might want to cancel, or you might instead revolve the lesson around the occasion.

Give your child a notebook. In it she can record what is taught in class, as well as rituals and prayers you teach her. Then she will be able to perform them on her own.

Begin each lesson with a short (five minutes or less) period of meditation. There are many kinds of meditation that will work. The idea here is to quiet the child and establish that this is a special time. Guided meditation works better than formless kinds with children. A centering prayer such as the one in Chapter 6 that begins "Here in the center of the world I stand" is another good beginning.

Guided meditations bridge the gap between the instruction required by a beginner and the imagination desired in the more advanced. They do this by providing a description of a journey or image, while leaving parts to the meditator.

Many books and tapes give texts for guided meditation. I have given one for an encounter with the Goddess, with an emphasis on the child forming his own image, and one for encountering the God, where the image is more defined.

Encountering a deity is a common use for guided meditations. They can be incorporated into classes presenting particular deities. You can write your own with a little research. After choosing a deity, read the relevant myths and seek out photographs or drawings of images to determine the deity's appearance, as well as the types of scene in which he or she might be found and what teaching will be imparted.

As with all meditation, the goal is to be both relaxed and alert. Start with whatever meditation work you usually do. Then read the text in a slow soft voice. When the meditation is over, it is best for the meditator to remain for a while in the same position, breathing slowly, before ending.

A Goddess Guided Meditation

This can be done before making an image of the Goddess or simply to help the child in his devotions. Its goal is to form an image of the

Goddess in the child that will help him imagine her more clearly. In the course of it, the Goddess gives a teaching that will be unique each time it is done.

Have the child sit in a comfortable position. His back should be straight. Read the text slowly, pausing to give him time to think when it is called for.

We are going to imagine the Great Mother.
It is good to imagine.
Imagination is halfway to magic.
If you keep imagining the Goddess you will find
   She becomes real and then your imagining
   will have become real.
You will have built her a road to come to you on.
She is everything, of course:
Maiden, Mother, Crone.
Today we are going to imagine the Mother.
Think of her.
She is strong.
She is beautiful.
She is peaceful.
She is smiling.
Ask yourself questions and put the answers
   in the image.
Is she sitting or standing?
Is she wearing clothes or is she naked?
Does she have jewelry?
What color is her hair?
How long is it?
Is it curly or wavy or straight?
How is it worn?
What color is her skin?
What color are her eyes?
What do you see in them?
Is her nose small or large?
Hooked or straight?
Wide or narrow?
Are her lips large or thin?
Are they dark or light?
Are her breasts large or small?
What shape are they?
Are her hips narrow or wide?

How does she hold her hands?
Does she hold anything in them?
She says something to you.
What is it she says?
If you can't hear her, that is OK.
You can feel something, even if it isn't in words.
She loves you.
She has the strength to help you.
It is yours when you want it.
When you are afraid
or worried
or just need a hug
and no one is around to help you
imagine her
and she will hold you in her arms.
Hold her image for a few more seconds
and then thank her and say goodbye.
Let the image fade away
But don't worry.
She is still with you.
She is everywhere.
Always.

A God Guided Meditation

In this type of guided meditation the meditator is given very specific imagery and a particular message. The point is to convey what sort of imagery and teaching is associated with a particular deity. To use this type with a child requires you to be sure of these yourself.

Imagine that you are in the woods.
The trees around you are pines.
There is just enough light to see by, but it comes to
    you from above the branches of the trees.
The trees are very tall, and their branches don't
    start until very high up, higher than a house.
Everything around you smells like pine.
The ground is covered with needles.
The trunks of the trees rise from those needles,
straight and tall and rough and hard.
You can hear birds in the branches,
    but you can't see them.
Except for the birds, there is no noise at all.

*Sit for a second and imagine the trees and the birds
and the quiet.*

(Pause)

*From somewhere in front of you, you start to hear
a sound.
It is the sound of a drum beating.
It beats in time with your breathing.
As you pay attention to it, it starts to sound louder,
and now you can tell that it comes from exactly
in front.
Walk towards the drum.
As you walk, you find the way is easy.
There seems to be a path between the trees.
Maybe deer have made it.
The path leads just the way you are going.
The pine needles on the ground are soft,
like a carpet, so you take off your shoes and socks
and walk in your bare feet.
You keep walking through the woods.
The trees are still pines, but they start to grow
closer together.
You keep walking, and soon they are so close
together that you can't fit between
them anymore.
It's as if they have grown together into a wall.
So you start to follow the wall to your left.
It starts to curve, and you realize it makes a circle.
You look closely at it as you walk, and you notice
that in some places it is not so solid.
In fact, you find a place where, if you try real hard,
you might be able to just barely squeeze through.
It looks hard, but you are brave,
so you push yourself through.
On the other side of the wall is a clearing.
It's still a little dark, but if you look straight up
you can see the sky,
and in the middle of the sky is a single star.
In the center of the clearing is a small hill.
In the side of the hill is a small cave.
You go to the mouth of the cave and look inside.
There is a man sitting there looking at you.*

He is sitting crosslegged on the ground.
He has antlers growing from his head.
His hair is rough and shaggy.
He is wearing pants that seem to be made of leather,
but his chest and feet are bare.
Now you notice he is smiling.
On his lap is a bag of coins.
He takes one out and gives it to you.
On one side of it is a picture of the man.
On the other side is the name "Cernunnos."
Of course, he is not a man; he is a god.
In fact, he is the *God, the one who is the father*
of everything.
He says, "Keep this coin, and when you want to
feel me near you, just imagine you are holding
it in your hand."
You thank him, and then he starts to fade away.
Around you the cave is also fading away,
and the wall of trees, and the woods.
You find yourself right back in your own home,
back where you started.
You open your eyes, and here you are.
But in your pocket, you can feel the coin.

Follow the meditation with a talk on a particular subject. If the meditation has been a guided journey, with contact with a deity or other spiritual being, you will want to talk about that. If possible, include something for the child to do as part of this.

End the lesson with a myth, fairy tale, or folk tale, preferably one that is told rather than read. Don't limit yourself to one tradition; there are many cultures that can be learned from. The myth might not be connected with the day's lesson, since there are so many important myths and many of them overlap.

Sometimes renting a video can take the place of a class. Many movies play with mythical themes. Most of them draw from hero myths—*Star Wars*, *The Never Ending Story*, *Camelot*, etc. Joseph Campbell and Bill Moyers' "Power of Myth" series is available on tape and can be used for older children.

Don't forget extracurricular activities. Trips to museums, nature centers, the beach, the woods, or even just a walk can be used to supplement a lesson or even to replace it for a week. Older children should be given practical living-in-the-world assignments to teach them to live out their Paganism. Examples would be recycling, composting, volunteering, helping teach other children, taking care of an animal, etc.

Sample Lessons

Take two pieces of paper and draw a line across the top of each. Above the line write on one "Goddess Woman Mother" and on the other "God Man Father." Ask your child to think, during the next week, about what comes to mind when they think of those words, and to write these things down. They don't necessarily have to write them under the exact word that they associate with them. Use these as points of discussion when presenting, the next week, the attributes of the God and Goddess.

Explain the three phases of the Goddess. (See Chapter 8.) Take as many pictures and figures of goddesses as you can find and explain them. After each is explained have the child sort it by which phase it most fits. Have her explain her choices.

Make a list of all-purpose God and Goddess names (names that refer to the God and Goddess as a whole rather than to their aspects). Explain them and have the child pick one of each to use in self-blessing exercises.

Choose about a dozen gods and goddesses. Over the course of several months, teach about them, one at a time. Give their functions and explain how they can be called upon. Give attributes and descriptions to help the child visualize them better. You can make pictures of them. If possible, teach about each of them at an appropriate place: Manannan at the seashore, Demeter in a garden, Thor under an oak tree.

After the series is over, ask your child to pick one of the deities you have discussed. With your child, build a shrine to this deity and devise rituals to worship him or her.

⚛ 6 ⚛

Prayers and Offerings

Prayer is a loaded word. Our childhood memories of prayer are sometimes unpleasant. Even the pleasant ones can cause problems for Pagans if they bring up Judeo-Christian images. But remember two things. First, prayer is a perfectly Pagan thing to do. Don't limit your religion in reaction to your childhood. Second, your children don't have any childhood memories yet. It's up to you to make sure the ones they develop are good ones. Don't limit *their* religion in reaction to *your* childhood.

It's worth looking at some of the objections raised to prayer. Perhaps if they are understood, prayer can be redeemed not only for our children's sake but for ours as well.

For instance, prayer is often criticized as a rote activity. We all remember praying almost mindlessly, without paying attention to the meaning of the words. But what is wrong with that? Isn't that what we do when we chant? Is it really so much better to consciously dwell on the meaning of every word? Even a superficial glance through techniques used by the world's religions, even the Pagan ones, will turn up a variety of rote techniques—mantras and rosaries, for instance. The lack of conscious effort allowed by memorized prayers can shut our minds up long enough to allow the sacred in, if we give it a chance. Further, rote prayers are uniquely consoling in tragic circumstances. When something terrible has happened to us, it is a great comfort not to have to think of words to express our emotions. A well-worn prayer comes to our lips, and we start to feel better.

Another common objection is to petitionary prayer. "Our relationship with the gods shouldn't include the word 'gimme'." Or "They turn the sacred into a cosmic Santa Claus." Well, perhaps they do. But you grew out of it; trust that your children will too.

Of course, sometimes children get into the habit of using prayer as a shopping list. Then, when the prayers are not answered, they turn off to religion, without even asking whether their prayers were appropriate in the first place.

The old Pagan concept of petition was expressed in the Roman "do ut des"—I give that you might give. The Pagan doesn't say "gimme." She says, "Here I am, doing what is right to do. Now you do what is right to do." And after the prayer is fulfilled, she thanks the gods. So a Pagan petitionary prayer teaches personal responsibility and gratitude, not cosmic materialism.

Petitionary prayer can be a wonderful thing for a child. Children often feel helpless when loved ones are suffering. They are often too young to help by either material or magical means. But if they can pray, then they can help. Prayer can also reinforce caring for others, if they do not pray only for themselves.

Prayers of praise and presence are an introduction to what may later become mysticism. Prayers to sacred spots, trees, rocks, animals, and other natural features teach respect for the world. They say, "The world does not belong to humans alone."

Prayers for children are best short and poetic. If they rhyme or have a strong meter they are easier for children to memorize. A singsong effect which might repel adults is often loved by children. Here are some sample prayers:

Prayer to Establish Sacred Space

Here in the center of the world I stand,
earth is before me,
air on my right hand,
fire is behind me,
on my left water lies,
as I stand here between
the earth and the skies.

Prayers to the Goddess

Mother of All
Queen of the Earth
Here I am,
One of your children.
Help me to be
the best I can be
so that people will know
the wonder of you.

She's with me
and hugs me
and loves me
and keeps me
as safe as can be
my Goddess, my Mother.

I'm with her
and hug her
and love her
and keep her
inside in my heart
my Goddess, my Mother.

Thank you, dear Mother,
for giving us birth.
Thank you, dear Goddess,
the Great Mother Earth.

The bright moon above me shines her soft light
and kisses me standing here hugged by the night.

Morning Prayers

Good morning, world, and good morning, sun.
I greet the new day with my arms spread wide
and thank the gods for the dreams they sent.

It's daytime again,
and time to get up.
Look down on me, Sun,
as I go through my day.
Help me to learn
and be good
and be kind
to all of the people.
I meet on my way.

Mealtime Prayers

Eating is a sacred act. By eating we take part in the mysteries of life and death. It is especially incumbent on meat eaters to remember those that have died to make their food, but even vegetarians take lives in order to live. That is the way it is.

Prayer before meals is thus always appropriate, although you may wish to have a short version for everyday use and a longer one for special occasions such as festivals, moon observances, or a weekly family night meal. Here are some simple mealtime prayers:

We thank the spirits of the land
who gave us this food.
We thank the women and men
who grew it and prepared it.
We thank the Lady and Lord:
We bless this food in their names.

Food is the gift of the Earth,
Warmed and lit by the Sun
Coming from the Goddess
by the power of the God:
We are blessed by eating it.

We thank the plants and animals
whose deaths make our lives
We thank the God and Goddess
Who bring death and life.

Here before us on the table
are great gifts.
Born from the Mother
Shaped by the Father
Prepared by human hands
to be our food.
We thank those who brought them to us.

Isn't it wonderful?
Look at this food.
Where did it come from?
How did it get here?
The Earth gave birth to it.
The Sun fed it.
The waters filled it.
People cared for it.
And when it was time,
it was harvested.
People prepared it
and now it is here for us.
Thank you, Earth.
Thank you, Sun.
Thank you, waters.
Thank you, people.

Blessings to the Spirits of the Land.
Blessings to the Guardians of our family.

Blessings to the Lady and the Lord.
Blessings upon the food we will eat tonight.

For special occasions a more complex grace might be desired. Before the meal, prepare as much of the food as possible as a family. Set the table with special dishes and linens. Put candles in the center, with a bell next to them. When everything is ready, ring the bell (a child can do this) to mark the beginning of sacred time. When the sound has all died away, light the candles, saying:

In the light of these flames
there is peace.
May all on whom they shine be blessed.

Follow this with one of the short prayers. Put a small portion of each food on a plate to be put in the family shrine later as an offering. Alternatively, one of the children could bring the plate to the shrine at this time. As you place the food on the plate, say:

We share our fortune with our household guardians.

At the end of the meal, blow out the candles and ring the bell to signal the end of special time. Then everybody should help clean up.

Bedtime Prayers

The Great Horned Lord,
the bringer of dreams,
rides through the night
on roads of moonbeams.
Please give me your gifts
of visions and sight
as I lie in my bed
asleep in the night.

Lord of Dreams
I pray to you
at the end of the day.
Lady of Sleep

I pray to you
at the start of the night.
Send me sleep
and send me dreams
restful and sweet
till I wake up again.

Lord of Dreams
send me sweet dreams
Lady of Night
send me sweet sleep.
Lord and Lady
Hold me in your arms
until morning comes
and I wake up again.

Mother of Everything, wrap me in your arms,
and carry me off to the land of dreams.

As I go to sleep I think of all the others
with whom I share this world
and I ask the Mother
and I ask the Father
to bless them all and make them happy.

Blessed be the Mother.
Blessed be the Father.
Blessed be all their children everywhere.

Blessings

When a member of the family is leaving the home, whether to move out or just for a long trip, he should be blessed by the parents. This extends the protection of the gods and the household guardians over him while he is gone. The blessing may include the name of a deity of travelers such as Woden or Hermes, or one who is a protector, such as Isis or Mithras.

Someone moving out will need to tell the guardians and leave an offering. The person giving the blessing holds her hands over the head of the person receiving the blessing while saying the words. These should be suited to the person and the occasion. Here are some examples:

May She bless you while you are far from home
May He guide you on your way
May you return in safety to your home
to those who love you and wait for you.

The blessings of Woden upon this traveler.
May he make your path clear before you
and smooth out difficulties before they arise.

Our Lady Isis wraps her wings around you:
Rest securely in them,
and know you will be safe.

You go on your way to see many new things.
Do not waste this chance to learn of the world.
Keep your eyes open.
Keep your ears ready.
And return better than you left.
You go under the protection of the gods
and the hands of the guardians will be with you
wherever you go.

I bless you with the blessing of our Lady.
I bless you with the blessing of our Lord.
I send you on your way marked with their sign
that all who meet you might know of their power.
Remember, you are their child:
Do nothing to shame them.
They will not forsake you.

I call upon the guardians of our family
to keep their protection over this family member
who will be away from our home.
He may go far from the shrine of the guardians,
but they will continue to watch over him.

No matter where you travel it will be on the Earth.
No matter where you travel it will be under the Sky.
They will watch over you
They will care for you
They will not forget you
They love you with a parent's love
as we love you with a parent's love.
Our blessing goes with you.

You are going into the place of another people,
a place with its own guardians, its own spirits,
    its own gods.
Yours will go with you.
Greet theirs with respect and reverence.
May they be your friends even as the Gods
    of this place are.

Offerings

The giving of offerings to gods, spirits, and ancestors is an ancient practice that may well be the most common religious act in the world. Many of the treasures we have from ancient cultures, especially from the Celts, were offerings that were buried or thrown into water. The Battersea shield, the Gundestrup cauldron, the statues from the source of the Seine—what wonderful devotion is expressed in the giving of these masterpieces to the gods. And how many more humbler offerings of food and drink must have been made!

An offering can sometimes be in the nature of a business deal—I give you this, O god; now you give me that. It is perhaps not the most mature of relationships with the sacred, but it has many years of tradition to back it up. The gods appreciate justice, and will acknowledge fair dealings.

An offering may mean other things, though. It may be saying to the god, "See; you're important to me, important enough that I am willing to give up these things for you." It may be an expression of gratitude, an acknowledgement of indebtedness. "I know I got what I got with your help, so this is your share." And, like all exchanges, it can help establish or solidify a relationship. "We give each other things; that's what friends do."

Offerings can be made of many different things. They can be libations poured on the ground, food, incense, and even hair. Hair is a common gift to ancestors—we recognize that our bodies come from them, so we give some of that body back. It is especially suitable for offerings at rites of passage: we give up part of ourselves as a sign that the old us is passing away. The cutting of hair is also traditional as a sign of mourning (with the death of a loved one we have lost a piece of ourselves). All grains are good, as is prepared food and drink. Artwork, a song, our time and labor—anything of value to us is worthy of being used as an offering.

A table of suggested offerings for different kinds of spirits and deities is given in Appendix 2. These are drawn from many cultures. An investigation of these cultures turns up patterns. Certain types of spirits prefer certain types of gifts. Location plays a part as well. American nature spirits are fond of cornmeal and tobacco, both from plants that originated in this country.

If there are specific deities you wish to offer to but do not know the favored offerings for, there are three courses open to you. First, you could offer what my daughter calls "the usual"—grain (preferably cooked by you, so as to add your own gift) and beer or wine. Second, you can do some research. The references list some places to start. The best beginning is with *The Funk & Wagnall Standard Dictionary of Folklore, Mythology, and Legend*. You will need to go on from there. Third, you could ask the deity or spirit concerned. Follow the same steps as for making an offering, but when you reach the part where the actual offering would be given, instead ask the deity what he or she would like. Listen carefully, with intuition as well as ears, and if you receive an answer thank the deity and go get the requested item. Return and start the offering again.

The general procedure for making offerings is simple. First stand or sit for a few moments, dwelling on the sacredness of the spot. All spots are sacred. Some appear to be more than others—an ancient tree, a weathered stone, the border between our yard and our neighbor's, our stove as it cooks our food. But the lack of sacredness we perceive in other places is in ourselves, not in those places. We are blind to their holiness.

The way to overcome this blindness is to open our eyes, to really open our eyes. What we see usually is as dependent on what we expect as on what is there. To see the sacred in every spot we must stop our expectations and judgements and let the spot be what it is.

Pay attention to the spot, but without making any judgements, even to the extent of naming what happens. For instance, suppose a wasp flies by. Don't think, "Wasp—I'm afraid of them." Don't think, "Wasp—important for pest control." Don't even think, "Wasp." Just let the wasp fly by, being what it is. This is the way to honor a spot, by allowing everything in it to be what it is without interference.

After you have honored the spot, you can start to call the spirit you are going to offer to. You can do this out loud, calling the spirit's name or title. (Many spirits, especially nature spirits, have no names, at least none they will tell us.) You can also do it silently, concentrating on a mental picture of the spirit. These two ways can be combined.

Once you can feel the presence of the spirit, place the object to be offered. If you do not feel the spirit, you can place the offering whenever it feels right. Sometimes the very act of giving the offering will bring a spirit to you.

Whatever words you are using may be said before, during, or after the offering is placed. What you say will vary with your intent, with the spirit to whom the offering is made, and with your relationship with that spirit. A typical offering prayer is:

> *We give of ours.*
> *You give of yours.*
> (The spirit's name or title), *here is a gift.*
> *I am your friend.*
> *Be my friend, too.*

After the offering is placed, sit or stand a moment or two, again dwelling on the sacredness of the spot. Thank the spirit for its attention and leave respectfully.

Offerings given indoors may be placed or poured into bowls. These can be special bowls used only for this and kept in the household shrine or you can use your everyday bowls or your best china. Allow the offerings to stay for at least 24 hours and then remove them to outdoors. They can be taken to your yard, a roadside, or a river, lake, or harbor.

Teach your children to make offerings. Explain why offerings are made, make a few with them, and make sure there are suitable items available to them for them to offer on their own. Whenever a ritual calls for an offering, consider allowing them to make it.

✿ 7 ✿

The Festivals

All religions have sacred days. What sets the Pagan holy days apart from those of the rest of the Western religions is that they do not celebrate historical events. They celebrate themselves. What is special about this day is that it is this day. A Pagan lives in the world and finds religious meaning in the events of the world. The most radical and at the same time most enduring of these events are those concerned with seasonal change and so Pagans build our lives around them and celebrate their turning points.

Some have thought that Pagans believed that without their rituals the seasons would not change. Perhaps some Pagans have believed this. But what really matters is that Pagans and the world are doing the same thing. Whether there is cause and effect is irrelevant. We do what we do because it is right for us to do it. We pattern our lives around the pattern of the seasons.

When we celebrate the festivals, we are honoring the seasons as we find them. We are recognizing them as sacred. But more than that, we are taking part in the continual creation of the Universe. It isn't something made long ago and then fixed in place, but a continual unfolding of the sacred. The Goddess is continually giving birth to the world, and we are Her midwives as well as Her children.

As the seasons change they turn the Wheel of the Year. This is the Neo-Pagan term for the seasonal changes when seen as a whole. Many Pagans have a particular form of the Wheel, expressed as a myth. These myths vary from group to group, but usually contain elements in common: the birth of the Sun, marriage of Goddess and God, death of the God, battle between Winter and Summer or the waxing and waning years.

Whatever form of the myth is used, however, the particular days celebrated by North American Neo-Pagans are generally those of Wicca. The Wiccan sacred calendar has eight holy days or festivals: Samhain (Halloween), Yule (Winter Solstice), Imbolc (February 2nd), Ostara (Spring Equinox), Beltane (May Day), Midsummers (Summer Solstice), Lammas (August Eve), and Harvest (Fall Equinox). In Figure 2, Yule is at the top and the others of course go clockwise. This is the skeleton of the year; celebrating it is the flesh.

The Wiccan calendar is usually described as Celtic and there are indeed strong Celtic elements in it. The Gaels certainly celebrated four of the festivals. (The evidence for the other Celts is sketchy, although they seem to have celebrated at least some of the four.) The solstices and the Fall Equinox were a later addition to British Paganism, however, brought in by the Romans and the Saxons. The Spring Equinox may have been introduced by the Romans, it may have been introduced for symmetry with fall, or it may have been modeled on Easter. Yule is definitely Saxon, and Midsummers almost certainly so, although there is a small chance it was celebrated by the Britons. There were further influences by Vikings and Christians. Modern Pagans have added elements from Greece and the Ancient Near East.

British Paganism had many mothers, then, and more have been added since. And to an even larger extent, so too does American Neo-Paganism. That is one reason these festivals draw from many traditions, going beyond their British origins, and even beyond Europe, to include customs from the whole world. There is always room to draw from more. Although for most of us our ancestors are Indo-European and we are most comfortable with Indo-European ways, further back all people are one people, and the wisdom of any may be appreciated by all.

Figure 2. The Wheel of the Year

These rituals are written for a northern temperate climate, the one in which the British Wheel of the Year developed. If you live in a different climate please do not celebrate them on the traditional dates. Meditate on the meaning of each festival and choose a date which corresponds locally to that meaning. Coordinate the festival with other local Pagans if possible. Remember, the whole point of being a Pagan is to be in tune with Nature. That's hard to do if your calendar is out of whack.

I remember celebrating May Day in Gulfport, Mississippi, with a Maypole and ritual combat between Winter and Summer.

There we were, celebrating the beginning of a season that had actually begun a month and a half earlier. It just didn't work.

If you feel that you must celebrate the traditional dates (and the solstices and equinoxes certainly deserve to be celebrated) change the rituals to reflect the season where you are. What is going on at your time and your place? That is what you must celebrate.

A common mistake made in interpreting seasonal customs of other cultures is to look at the date on the calendar instead of the seasons of the place where the customs originated. This has waylaid many, for instance, into thinking that the dying and resurrecting god of the ancient Near East (Tammuz, Adonis, et al.) was a god of spring. His festival does occur near the Spring Equinox, it is true, and there is much equinoctial symbolism in his myth and cult. But in the area where he was worshiped the Spring Equinox is the time of the barley harvest, not the return of life after death and cold. Rituals inspired by his myths would therefore be more appropriate in our fall. For this reason, some of the suggestions for celebrating these festivals that have been taken from cultures in different climates have been shifted away from their traditional calendar dates. Your rituals should reflect nature's calendar, not Pope Gregory's.

Look around you for other days that should be celebrated. My family has been known to celebrate baseball's opening day. (Well, the Yankees' opening day, to be precise.) If you live in a fishing community, what are its major days? If you farm, when are your crops planted and harvested? Pagans in a community that relies on skiers for its livelihood might well celebrate the first snowfall. Paganism has a long history of supporting the economic well-being of its followers.

Think also about what secular holidays (Valentine's Day, St. Patrick's Day, Memorial Day) are near the festivals and what can be incorporated. Don't forget non-Pagan celebrations in your community. Some of these have a long history (harvest fairs, for instance), while others are more recent (First Night celebrations in many American cities), but they are all responses by people to the seasons. And indeed, consider celebrating secular holidays in a Pagan way. They are part of our culture and reflect the changing of the seasons.

Few Neo-Pagans grew up in our religion. But we did grow up in a different kind of household, for most of us a Christian one, that did certain things for certain days. Many of these things are Christian adaptations of Pagan customs. This is not to say that all Christian customs were stolen from us. There are certain characteristics shared by all humans and because of this certain symbols will call to them no matter what religion they are. The local versions of these symbols will vary, but the truth behind them will not.

To see what these basic symbols are, think of your own childhood. I grew up Roman Catholic, so let me use that as an example. The biggest festival for me as a child was, of course, Christmas. When I think of Christmas I think of decorations, foods, family gatherings, and presents. I don't think of ritual words. It is a mistake to take mystery rites and adapt them for home use. After all, Roman Catholics don't say masses in their homes. And the Pagans of old didn't celebrate the mysteries with their families.

Emphasize the importance of foods, decorations, clothing; things you *do*, not things you say, then. Think about your own childhood and what things were important about holidays and incorporate them into your celebrations.

For some of the festivals, the most important element in Pagan times seems to have been a feast. This is certainly Pagan; eating is a sacred act. An air of festivity surrounded the feasts, with games and songs. Were there rituals as well? We don't know. There are in modern Pagan festivals, but they must never take the place of the feast.

The importance of traditional foods cannot be overemphasized. In my house when I was growing up it just wouldn't have been Christmas without certain kinds of cookies. Children can help with food preparation and learn useful skills while having fun celebrating the seasons.

Decorations provide both an air of festivity and a constant reminder of the occasion. Children can help make them and they can help put them up. Seasonal decorations that can be made by children are found in magazines and teachers' resource books. (See References and Resources.) Making them is a great way to teach the significance of the occasions.

Seasonal flowers are always appropriate as decorations. These are simply the flowers in bloom at the time you are celebrating. I cannot give a list that would be appropriate everywhere this book may be used, so you will have to go out looking for them. Take your child with you and she may learn something. The flowers may be grown in your yard or a window box, or they may be gathered from along roads.

Don't neglect "weeds." Plants are only weeds where they are not wanted. A sure sign of late spring are the dandelions brought home by schoolchildren everywhere as gifts for their parents. If you can gather wildflowers you will always be sure of having the right ones for the season and the change of flowers from festival to festival will reinforce the message of the changing of the seasons. After the holiday they can either stay where they are until they die completely (and then onto the compost heap with them) or they can be placed in your shrine. In the winter you can use bare sticks or evergreen branches.

As one exception to the seasonal rule, branches with buds can be cut in the spring, brought inside, and forced. This could even be seen as a kind of magic to bring in the change of season.

On all festivals, only necessary work should be done. This is standard practice for holy days; "holiday" originally meant "holy day." In our predominantly Christian society, for instance, very few places of business are open on Christmas. Similarly, in ancient Rome no public business could be performed on the major religious holidays. And in old Ireland it was traditional to avoid all work that involved turning—spinning, driving of carts, etc. Perhaps this was an attempt to keep the holiday for as long as possible, before the Wheel of the Year turned and went on to less special days.

On the other hand, there is no ban on fun of any kind on these days. Besides rituals, food, and decorations, find fun things to do. Do them as a family. For all four of the solar festivals, the solstices and equinoxes, the traditional symbol is the wheel or the ball, the sun brought down to earth. So depending on the season, try whiffleball, throwing disks, bicycling, roller skating, volleyball, sledding in plastic saucers, marbles, or bowling. Go to an amusement park and ride the great wheels of light—the merry-go-rounds, ferris wheels, and those large drums that spin around so fast that you don't fall even when they tip. (The ones my mother would never let me go on because she said they were too dangerous.)

Clean your house for the festivals. This is especially important for Samhain, Yule, and Brighid's Day, when someone is being invited into your home. The effort expended in cleaning is an offering, and the clean house is a sign of respect towards your guests.

The rituals for the solar festivals use a sun candle. It is the thread that ties the solar rituals together. It is a large candle that is a solar color (red, yellow, orange, or gold). Since it is used on four different festivals, an unscented one is best. A scent which would fit perfectly with one of the festivals might clash with another. Decorate its base for each of its days—holly, flowers, leaves, and fruit or grain. A design such as a sun can be cut into it with a hot knife. Keep it in your shrine when not in use, where it can double as an image of the God.

Some of these rituals use fires, either bonfires or barbecue fires. Offerings can be made to (or through) the fire, a sort of sacrifice. Give a portion of your own food and a bit of your own drink so the fire can share the feast with you. The ashes from the fire should be put on your garden if you have one. They may also be given to trees or sprinkled around the outside of the house to protect it. (Ashes from barbecue briquets are not good as fertilizer.)

Before having a bonfire, check with your local authorities to make sure it is allowed and safe. Some towns require permits. Be sure the ground under the fire is free of anything that might burn, and clear an area around the fire as well. Surround the fire with a circle of rocks to further keep in the burning wood. Make sure you have buckets of water or sand, or a fire extinguisher handy in case the fire gets out of control.

When the fire is out, make sure it is all the way out before leaving it by soaking it with water, stirring it, soaking again, and then checking with your hand for hot spots. To do this, run you hand over the ashes (don't actually touch them), stir the ashes, and repeat. Don't leave the fire untended until you are sure it is out. Starting forest or brush fires will not make friends for Pagans either with the spirits of the wild or our neighbors.

Some of these rites may best be performed on the eve of the day. Night can be considered to have begun the moment the first star can be seen, or if the horizon can be seen from your home, the family can watch the sunset before starting the ritual.

Samhain

Samhain (Halloween—October 31st) is more closely associated with Paganism than any other holiday. It has preserved many Pagan customs and more have grown up around it in Christian days. Indeed, unlike most Pagan occasions there are almost too many customs to integrate them all easily.

The Irish name Samhain, pronounced "Sowen" (the Scottish Gaelic is "Samhuin"), has been adopted by most American Neo-Pagans. The medieval Irish glossaries give its meaning as "summer's end," and that is its religious meaning among modern Pagans. Modern scholarship has cast doubt on this etymology, however. One recent suggestion is that it means "summer's beginning"—the summer of the Underworld, where the seasons are the opposite of ours. What is beyond doubt is that this day that begins the cold part of the year has "summer" in its name.

This is a good place to point out an error found in many books on Samhain that has unfortunately recently made its way into the Pagan community. "Samhain" is not the name of a Celtic god of the dead (a recent book said "Aryan"). Celtic gods are not as easily categorized as Greco-Roman, and if the Celts had a god of the dead it is unlikely that we will ever be sure who he was. But there was no god named "Samhain," or "Samana" as it is sometimes given.

"Samhain" properly refers to the daylight portion of the festival, to November 1st. The night of October 31st goes by a number of names—Oiche na Sprideanna (Spirit Night), Oiche Shamhna (Samhain Eve), Puca Night. It is a night of magic, when fairies and ghosts are about, and the puca spits on the blackberries, making them unfit to eat.

Among the Celts, as among the Hebrews and many others, the day began at sunset, with the dark time. The Celtic year also began with the dark—with Samhain. Just as a plant is born from the dark below the ground, so too the year comes from the dark time. Samhain is the Celtic New Year's Day, then.

The overwhelming cultural importance of the secular calendar has decreased the importance of the New Year aspect of Samhain for most Neo-Pagans. But if Samhain does not end the calendar year for us, it still marks the end of the year's growth. Not only does the world start to die, but it no longer grows to replace death. This is the end of the farmer's year. Cattle and sheep are brought in from the far pastures, winter wheat is already planted, wood is gathered.

Those of us who do not farm or even garden can use this time to wind up other things in our lives. For instance, debts can be paid if possible, to close the year so that a new one can begin free from connections to the old. Are there jobs around the house that you've been meaning to get to? Do them now, and free yourself to look forward instead of back.

Samhain eve is the night of death, when the fairy mounds open and the dead and the old gods walk the earth. Gifts of food and drink are left out for them, either in appeasement or greeting. It is the night when the veil is thin between our world and that of gods and spirits, and anyone may pass through either way.

Many Samhain customs are designed to protect the home from the spirits or the fairies. As Pagans we welcome the spirits and fairies, and so we do not keep some of these customs. Some of them we reinterpret. The jack-o'-lantern, far from scaring off spirits, may be seen as evidence of them in our midst.

It says in "The Wooing of Etain" that among the Irish Samhain was a day of peace, when no one could take arms against another. This is a characteristic law of tribal assemblies, and indeed, there is a slight possibility that "Samhain" means "assembly." Samhain is the great assembly day. If you are part of a Pagan group, gather them together for Samhain; if your extended family is Pagan, do likewise. If you have no group with which to assemble, do not worry. The spirits of your ancestors will gather with you. This is one time when Pagans do not stand alone.

In ancient Ireland, Samhain was actually part of a week long celebration, divided into three parts: the three days before it, the day itself, and the three days after it. The feast was long and well-celebrated.

In remembrance of this, your celebration should span at least three days. That is why there are three rituals given here. Unlike the other festivals, where several rituals are provided to give a choice, all three of these are meant to be performed, one on each of three days. It is best to perform them on consecutive days, but depending on local custom, you may have to reschedule one of the rituals so as not to conflict with trick or treating.

The origin of trick or treating has been the subject of a lot of speculation, some of it based on evidence and some not. I would not like to be one more person saying "this is how it began." I don't think we can know for sure.

What we can know is that everywhere in the ancient world the days before New Year's and feasts of the dead were days of ritual chaos. The world dissolved, the cosmos disintegrated, and the human community allowed itself to fall apart as well. There were celebrations with costume wearing, general lawlessness, children's revolts, and trick or treating. The meaning seems to have been that with the old year dying and the new one not yet begun the old rules are dead and new ones not yet in place. It is a time for both fear and merry-making. Pre-Ash Wednesday customs are probably the best known: Mardi Gras, Fasching, and Carnival.

We know that in the British Isles there are many customs associated with particular days that involve going from door to door collecting goodies: Pace Egging, Guy Fawkes, caroling, and, in areas influenced by Gaels (or, in modern times, by Americans), Halloween. These customs died out in America, but the influx of the Irish during the Potato Famine probably revived Halloween. This is conjecture, but the traditions are old and probably pre-Christian.

Secular Halloween customs are thus quite appropriate. Take part in them with a good conscience. As well as taking part in the local seasonal festivals, something that any self-respecting Pagan should be glad to do, and as well as giving your children the chance to feel that they are not that different from other children, something I'm sure most parents are glad to be able to do, you will be observing the Festival of the Death of the Year in traditional fashion. Go for it.

After the dissolution to chaos comes the re-creation of the world. This is the origin of the belief in many parts of the world that what happens on New Year's sets the pattern for rest of the year. One offshoot of this belief is the custom of practicing divination on days like this. The pattern of a thing is set at its beginning, so the year's pattern can be seen or altered by divination on Samhain.

Each of the three rituals deals with a different aspect of the day. First there is the seasonal aspect. This is the time of the year when things are dying. Even the plants that will survive the winter are shutting down and shedding unnecessary parts. Many animals, especially insects and spiders, don't survive the winter. The species overwinter as eggs or larvae.

In a pre-electricity culture even some of the domestic animals would be killed. There was only so much food and usually not all of the herds could be kept in good health until spring. As well as being carefully preserved for the winter, some of the food was used for a feast, not unlike the American Thanksgiving. On Martinmas (November 11th, and thus Halloween in the Julian calendar) farmers in Ireland killed an animal and sprinkled the blood on the threshold and the four corners for protection. The meat was shared with the poor.

Next there is the placating of the spirits of the animals eaten during the year. This is a recognition that we live by killing. Being a vegetarian is no way out of this, either. Life is life, and even vegetarians are responsible for death. In hunting cultures it is common to placate the spirits of the dead animals. This is partly to ensure their return and that they will continue to cooperate in the cycle of living and dying. But at least part of it is a recognition that the animals have a life that people take, and a spirit that deserves respect.

Third, there is the honoring of ancestors. Samhain is the night when the distinction between this world and the next is thin. Perhaps the fear of going out on this night arose not so much from concern about running into spirits of the dead as fear of crossing over into the Otherworld oneself.

A fourth aspect is the facing of personal mortality. This hardly seems appropriate for a gathering with children, however, but it is certain to be part of any meeting of adults or individual rites that may be held during this time.

The most effective way of scheduling these rituals would be to observe them in the order given here—plants, animals, people. This brings the message of Samhain closer to us personally each night. It should reach its crescendo on the night of Samhain itself, with only the grave visits left. Your scheduling may have to be different, but in any case the honoring of ancestors is best left for the night of Samhain itself.

On one or more of the days of observance it is appropriate to fast, except for the ritual itself. This is a custom often associated with New Year's days, as well as with preparations to meet with spirits. It fits in also with the coming of the hard times of winter, when in a subsistence culture going without food might be a necessity. Since the center part of each day's observance is a meal, fasting will also give greater emphasis to the ritual. If your family decides to fast, limit the fasting to healthy non-pregnant adults. Taking on the fast will be one of the responsibilities shared by those who have come of age. The money saved by fasting should be given to charity.

Pagans spend so much energy thinking about nature that it would be all too easy to forget about the human community. So on Samhain it is fitting to make a special act of charity. It has always been a day for giving, one where it is not proper to turn the stranger from your door. (Perhaps this is another theory of the origin of trick or treating. Samhain is the perfect day to ask for gifts; they will not be refused.) It is the end of harvest, when our storehouses are full and we can certainly spare some of our goods. We call to the ancestors and say, "Thank you for what you have done for us," and they say, "So, and what have you done for each other? And what have you done for your descendants?" If we are to face them without shame we must have an answer.

This is a time to clean your house extra well. You will be inviting the ancestors in, and simple politeness requires a clean house. But further, this is the new year: you should be able to face it with as little baggage from the old year as possible. In the same vein, wear new clothes for the rituals, especially for the night of the ancestors.

On the first day of the three, set up an extra table at one end of your kitchen or dining room table. Any size will do as long as it is at least as high as the other one (and preferably higher). This will serve as your Samhain altar. It will remain throughout the festival, decorated differently for each of the three days. Ordinarily your table serves as your altar, but for this special day a special altar is in order.

Decorations: Symbols of fall, harvest, and death, such as sickles, scythes, jack-o'-lanterns, skulls, skeletons, grave rubbings, root vegetables, squashes, and apples.

Food and drink: Dark food and foods that keep over the winter. Nuts, blackberries, applecakes, applesauce, roots, squashes, beef, pork, dark bread, mulled cider or wine.

Traditions to raid: All Saints Day (November 1st), All Souls Day (November 2nd), Martinmas (European; November 11th), Parentalia (February 13th-22nd), Fevalia (February 21st), Lemuralia (Roman; May 9th, 11th, and 15th), Bon (Japanese; August 13th-15th), Yom Kippur, Passover (Jewish; dates vary), Memorial Day, New Year's Eve.

The Night of Harvest's End

Prepare a meal that emphasizes vegetables and fruit. Include a heavy dark bread, a dark rye or pumpernickel, unsliced. This will be eaten from each night, so make sure there is some left over until the last night. Leave it on the altar for all three nights.

When the food is ready and the table set, gather the family together about it. After establishing sacred time, an adult says:

> *This is the first night of Samhain,*
> *Harvest's End.*
> *Summer is over and winter is upon us,*
> *the time to enjoy what our summer's work*
> *   has earned us*
> *and the time to prepare for summer's return.*
> *Blessed be winter, this sacred time of the year.*

Go out to your garden. Stand right in the middle of it, facing west, the direction of the dying sun and of the journey made by the dead. Make one last offering to the spirits of the garden (beer or wine are appropriate) and say:

> *Goodbye, summer.*
> *We have planted*
> *We have weeded*
> *We have harvested*
> *We have watched the garden*
> *and helped it grow*
> *and now its end has come.*

This would be a good point for the children to join in, thinking of things that have been done to help the garden and adding them to the list. If they have their own garden, they must perform this part of the ritual by themselves in that garden.

Then put the garden to sleep for the winter. Make the final harvest and pile the results in bowls. Pull up all the plants and haul them to your compost heap. Lay down mulch and compost. Then from some of the remains of the plants make a figure of a man. This will be your image of Winter. He will rule over your household until May Day. Those devoted primarily to the Goddess in her many forms may see this as Queen Winter, the Goddess as Hag or Cailleach.

To make the figure, make two bundles of stalks, one slightly thinner than the other but both the same length. The thinner bundle will be the arms. Be sure to include some of each plant. With a

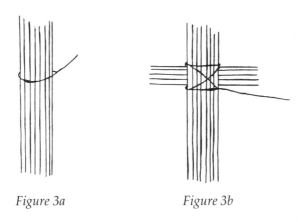

Figure 3a   *Figure 3b*

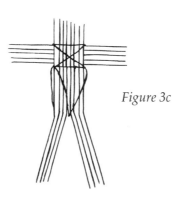

Figure 3c

Making Winter's Image

long piece of string, tie the large bundle together about one fourth of the way from one end (Figure 3a). This will be the head end. Separate the bundle slightly below the string and insert the smaller bundle. Wrap the string diagonally across and around to hold the arms in place (Figure 3b). Tie it off, leaving plenty of extra string. Spread the lower portion of the large bundle apart to form the legs. Run the string down through the dividing point, back up to one arm, down to the dividing point again, and back up to the other arm (Figure 3c). Pull the string tight to keep the legs divided and tie it off. You may also tie the ends of the bundles together if you wish. We like to keep ours rough, but you may make yours as elaborate as you care to.

Altar for the First Night of Samhain

If you grow corn your figure of Winter can be quite large. With different plants, you may need to make a smaller one. One to one and a half feet is a good size.

Put Winter in the north, the direction of dark, cold, and death. Face it and say:

Welcome, Winter.

If you don't have a garden you can find weeds along the road or in a vacant lot and make your figure of Winter out of them. Use dead and dry weeds, especially those with seeds in them. The first year my family did this ritual, we didn't have a garden, so we used dried grass from a nearby vacant lot. You will also need bowls of fruits and vegetables, preferably from local farms.

Bring Winter into the house with ceremony and place him at the table. Prop him to make him stand at his own place, with his own plate. The string that ties him together can be slipped over the top of a wine bottle to hold him up. Put your bowls of fruit and vegetables in front of him. Put bits of your food on Winter's plate as you eat, serving him first. Afterward leave the food out for the spirits of the wild or of the garden.

Keep Winter in a place of honor all winter until Beltane. If it is safe you could put him in the garden on a pole in the north to watch over the garden for the winter. If you do this, put the offerings of food in front of him.

This is the night for traditional Halloween games such as bobbing for apples or trying to eat donuts that are suspended on strings.

The Night of the Animal Spirits

If you keep any animals (including pets), no one may eat dinner until they are fed. Leave out food for wild animals as well.

Among the food include a soup containing a little bit of every food animal eaten during the year. Use any soup recipe with small pieces of the other animals added. Beef works well as the base, as its strong flavor is not easily overpowered by other meats. If you are vegetarian, make a soup using as many plants as possible and adapt the ritual accordingly. When everything is ready, establish sacred time. Then an adult says:

> *This is the second night of Samhain,*
> *the Night of the Animal Spirits.*
> *This is the night when we thank the animals*

who have died for us.
Blessed be the eaters
Blessed be the eaten
Blessed be the eating
Blessed be the being eaten
Blessed be life
Blessed be death.

The other family members repeat each of the "Blessed be's."
Then an adult says:

This is the great secret of life:
That it feeds on death
and they are close twins.
The wheel is always turning.
The spirits of the animals are here,
of all that we have eaten.
They have played their part
in the turning of the wheel
so tonight we do them honor.
Thank you.

All:

Thank you.

Adult:

Thank you.

All:

Thank you.

Adult:

Thank you.

All:

Thank you.

Adult:

> *Thank you, animal spirits,*
> *we will not forget your gifts.*

Serve the soup. Then eat your dinner, taking special care to taste and enjoy your food. Do not rush through the meal. That would be disrespectful to the animal spirits. Either make sure all leftovers are eaten or leave some out for the spirits. Whatever you do, don't waste any.

The Night of Remembering

The ancestors have been largely ignored by Neo-Pagans. Perhaps it's that we have been enraptured by the Celts and have associated ancestor religion with Africa, China, and Japan. Or maybe it's because so many of us have seen our path as breaking away from our family's religion. Or maybe it's just that Wicca lacks an emphasis on the ancestors. It is indeed ironic that those who seek to revive the ways of our ancestors have thought so rarely of the Way of the Ancestors.

But the ancestors are who we are. Their genes live in us, their culture shapes our days, their signs are all around us. The land itself speaks of them. And on the night of Samhain itself it is only right that we should speak of them as well. Speak, and remember. For what the ancestors desire most of all, and what we need most to do, is to remember them.

The meal on this night should include pork, the sacred feast animal of Northern Europe and food of the dead, apples, fruit of the tree that grows in the Otherworld, and the dark bread that has been on the table for the first two nights.

Decorate the room with symbols of your ancestors. These can include family trees, flags, postcards, foods, statues, books, photographs, or other items from the countries of your ancestors. Family heirlooms are also appropriate. These need not be anything fancy—a letter, a piece of clothing, a book—anything from any ancestor. (One of my favorite heirlooms is a hammer my grandfather used.) Photographs of ancestors can be used as well as rubbings or photographs of gravestones.

Altar of the Ancestors

This is a case where a cluttered altar is called for. Many sources have poured themselves into us and the result is a complicated culture filled with complicated people. Make your altar just as complicated. For tools, jewelry, and clothes raid your heirlooms and the traditions of your ancestors' culture.

Put images of your ancestors on the altar. If your household guardians are figures of your ancestors you will of course use them. If not, you could use masks made just for this rite, jack-o'-lanterns, or ethnic symbols. Set a place for them in front of their images. Also put on the altar a candle for each relative who has died since last Samhain, plus an extra candle for all your other ancestors. These candles can also be put in the window, to show the spirits the way to your home. Put any food that will be taken to the cemetery for an offering the next day in front of the images.

Dress in dark clothes. This is the night of the Underworld, the night world. Ordinarily we live in the day world, but this night we enter the world of the dark. The night world is the world of mystery, just like the world of death is. We cannot see what comes to us out of the dark.

Put the candles for the dead in front of the ancestral images. As you light each one that is being lit for a specific person, say that person's name. These candles should be lit by whoever in the family was closest to the person, although the oldest adult present presides this night. After the candles are lit, the oldest adult says:

Tonight is the last night of Samhain,
The Night of Remembering.
It is the feast of dark bread.
It is the feast of apples.
It is the feast of pork.
On this night
we welcome the spirits of our ancestors.
On this night
with the veil thin between the worlds
we welcome you to our house.
We share our meal with you
who have given us so much.

Put a bit of every food at the meal on the ancestors' plate as it is served, before serving any family members.

After the meal, clear the dinner dishes, except for the place of the ancestors. Put an apple, a pomegranate, a sharp knife, and a cup of dark wine or cider on the table. The wine or cider can be served mulled but cold by adding cloves and cinnamon sticks and soaking overnight. Stir or shake to mix the flavors before pouring. Pass the cup around. It may go either widdershins (thereby going down to death) or from youngest to oldest (thereby approaching the ancestors). Whichever way it goes, have it end up at the place of the ancestors.

As each person receives the cup she recites her genealogy, women and girls in the female line and men and boys in the male line. Say:

I am ( ), daughter of ( ), daughter of ( ).

Go as far back as you know or as you wish. Include at least one ancestor who is dead. If you do not know the names of your ancestors, at the point that the line disappears say, "daughter of a woman unknown." After each person does this, she drinks a toast in the direction of the place of the ancestors. When everyone has spoken and the drink and food are at the place of the ancestors, someone says:

We offer the cup of fellowship to the ancestors
They are dead but not gone.
We are all one people
and tonight we eat and drink together once more.

Someone else says:

We are not the first
We will not be the last
We are not the river's source
nor are we its end.
Life flows on
from the ancestors
through us
and beyond.
Daily we are carried along
as life streams on.
Tonight we turn and look upstream
and honor our source
before turning again
and plunging once more into life.
Tonight we remember our ancestors.
Gone but remembered.
Left but revered.
Away but near our hearts.
That which is remembered is still alive.
Those we remember are with us still.
We speak their names
and remember.

Then remember, saying their names. After each name, tell what you know about that person. If anyone has died since last Samhain, name him first. It is all right to call out the names of friends as well as family. We are one people.

There are many ancestors you will not know, of course. Call them by what you do know; where they came from, or what their trade was, or their relationship with you. There are many of mine of whom I know nothing except a name. That isn't really much, but it is enough.

Speak their names and remember them. When there are no more to remember, say:

> *Ancestors going back into the darkness,*
> *forgotten by history,*
> *your lives unrecorded*
> *You who are unknown to us*
> *but who made us ourselves.*
> *Don't be afraid:*
> *You are not forgotten.*
> *We remember you.*

And everyone says:

> *We remember you.*

Then tell any of your people's stories that haven't yet been told. Tell stories of ancestors who have died. Tell the old myths of your people. Recite the genealogies. And when the stories have died away, sit in silence and remember. Don't be afraid to cry. Your tears will be an offering to them. Don't be ashamed not to cry. The remembering may bring you comfort without the need to cry.

When the remembering has died away, someone says:

> *Every day we will remember*
> *and every night when we sleep.*
> *We will always remember*
> *and we will never forget.*
> *These are our people*
> *and we remember them.*

If you have any messages you wish sent to your ancestors, especially ones you don't wish to say out loud, write them down on a piece of paper. Put the paper with incense on a burning piece of charcoal, or burn them in the flames of the candles of the ancestors. The smoke will take your messages to the ancestors for you.

When all the talk is done and all the messages sent, the oldest adult says:

The table of remembering is over
but the Night of Remembering goes on.
But there is one thing more we still have to do.
For three days we have spoken of death:
of plants, of animals, of our ancestors.
But our way is life.

He picks up the pomegranate and says:

This is a fruit of life
It is filled with many seeds
But it was just these seeds that kept Persephone
    in the land of the dead.
So what does this fruit say to us?
It is life, whose shadow is death.

He cuts it open. Then he holds up the apple and says:

This is a fruit of death
It grows in the Otherworld where our ancestors live,
where they are rested and refreshed,
which is thus called the Land of Apples.

He cuts it through the middle horizontally and holds it up to show the star formed by the seed chambers. He says:

But hidden inside is the star of rebirth.
So what does this fruit say to us?
It is death, whose shadow is life
and promises rebirth.

He holds them both out and says:

Which is our way?
Which path are we on?
Are we on the path of death?
Or are we on the path of life?

All:

We are on the path of life.

He puts the fruits down and passes the pomegranate around so everyone can have at least one seed. He puts the apple back together and puts it on the altar and says:

> *And this is your path:*
> *Death, with the promise of rebirth.*
> *We say goodbye to you for now*
> *as you go your way*
> *and we go ours.*

Blow out the candles and share the pomegranate.

Samhain was one of the great bonfire days of the Gaels. Any of the festivals may be celebrated outside with a bonfire, and the Night of Remembering is particularly appropriate for its inside equivalent, the fire in the fireplace, where you may gather after the meal for more stories of the ancestors. On the first night, you might also light a bonfire in the garden or fields and carry fire around them to bless them.

Save the apple and the offerings on the ancestors' plate for the next day. The day of Samhain is as magical as the night. The door between the worlds is still open. Visit a cemetery. If possible, visit one where actual ancestors of yours are buried. If you can't do this, find the oldest one possible. Walk through it, reading the names on the tombstones out loud. Try to imagine who these people were. If your ancestors are buried there, point out their graves to your children and explain who they were and how they are related. Leave offerings, including the apple and the food from the ancestor's plate on some of the older graves, especially of your actual ancestors. Say:

> *We remember you,*
> *All our ancestors.*
> *See, here we are;*
> *We have not forgotten you.*
> *See, here are our gifts.*
> *We have not been idle.*
> *We have not wasted what you have left us.*

Any offerings in addition to the food from the previous night will depend on the culture you and they come from. In most cases some sort of bread and drink will be right. A common gift in Indo-European cultures is beans. Seeds of all sorts are appropriate as promises of rebirth. If you use drink, you may pour it on the ground. You may even wish to use hair, a part of you that is often given as an offering in rites. If you visit the graves of your own relatives you can leave offerings of their favorite foods or drawings made by your children.

Many cultures used what the British call "soulcakes"—small loaves made from the local grain. In India, they were made of rice. The Ainu of northern Japan used millet cakes. In parts of the British Isles, they were basically pancakes. In parts of Russia, gingerbread was used. The most traditional soulcake, therefore, is whatever bread, cake, or cookie you commonly eat. Pancakes, crepes, cornbread, pita bread, biscuits, Irish soda bread—what sort of cakes do you wish to share with your ancestors? What kind do you think they will like?

For a sweet soulcake with only three ingredients, try shortbread. It's easy to make:

4 oz. (1 stick) unsalted butter, softened
3 tbs. sugar
1 1/2 cups flour

Cream the butter and sugar together in a bowl. Sift the flour into the bowl and work until smooth. Divide the dough in half and shape each half into a circle about 1/2 inch thick. Place on an ungreased cookie sheet. Cut partially through into eight pieces and decorate with fork marks. Preheat oven to 375°. Bake for 10 minutes. Lower heat to 325° and bake for 20 minutes more. Cool.

As well as being given to the dead, soulcakes have been given to the poor and to children who come to the door. The first is an expression of the giving of the final harvest's bounty, and the second is yet another possible origin for trick or treating. Either may be a substitute for giving to the dead.

If you are from a culture that reveres its ancestors, research its rites. If, like the Chinese, your culture already has a day for revering the ancestors, perhaps you should perform these rites on that day. And of course, when looking at cultures to derive customs from, don't forget our own, with its wreaths and flowers.

Yule

Yule is the winter solstice, which, because the calendar year and the solar year are not exactly the same, can be on different days in different years. It is always near December 21st, though, and a calendar or almanac will give the exact day and time.

"Solstice" means "the sun stands still." Since Midsummers the sun has been rising and setting further south and thus staying lower in the sky and for a shorter time each day. Now we start to wonder: will this continue? Will the Earth grow darker and colder as the sun disappears into the south until only darkness is left?

But on Yule a wonderful thing happens. The sun stops its decline and for a few days it rises in about the same place. This is the crucial time, the cusp between events. The sun stands still, and everyone waits for the turning.

In our heads we know the light will return. But in the dark of winter, can we be sure? Do our hearts believe what our heads tell us? Will light keep its promises? We all have moments of darkness, when we don't know how much deeper we will go before the light starts to return (or even if it will). The world has its moments too; it understands us, and lives as we do.

The sun does start north again and the light comes back. In the world, in our lives, the light comes back. This is indeed something worth celebrating, and it has been celebrated throughout the Northern Hemisphere in remarkably similar ways.

The most important part of the celebration is light, in all its forms—Yule logs, bonfires, Christmas trees, Kwanzaa candles, Menorahs. The meaning of the lights varies from culture to culture and even from person to person. They can be magic to help the sun's return, a sign of hope in the dark and cold, a symbol of the Unconquerable Sun to cheer us, or a festival multiplication of the necessary lights of dark times. But then, Paganism is a religion of doing, not believing, and so what matters is that you do what should be done for Yule. Bring back the light in your home and know that it will also be coming back in the world.

The word "Yule," according to Bede, means "Wheel." It was "Guili" back then. We don't know whether it was meant to refer to the wheel of the sun or the turning of the Wheel of the Year, but either would be appropriate. It apparently meant the entire season, the last month of one year and the first of the next. Most recent scholars have been less certain and are more like to give its origin as simply "Germanic, original meaning unknown." We are lucky to have "Yule" though, no matter what its original meaning; it is a short friendly word that fits well into our language. It is familiar even to non-Pagans through songs, originally written for Christmas, that use it and that can be adopted by Pagans.

Many Christmas customs are derived from Yule customs. The tree, the Yule log, wreaths, lights, fires—all have their origin in Pagan Midwinter customs.

Yet as we have them, these customs are definitely Christian. The Christmas tree as we know it was not put up by the Pagans of old. It is true that northern Europeans decorated their homes with pine boughs and that Romans hung trees with masks and fruit in honor of the new year. Still, the modern Christmas tree is the result of years of development within a Christian framework. Because of this, some may wish to skip it (especially people who grew up as non-Christians), or they may wish to return to a simpler, more Pagan version.

Others may choose to adopt the whole set of decorations and customs, even those that had no Pagan origin, with suitable thanks for the creativity of Christianity. There is no reason why these symbols of life in death and light out of darkness cannot be used both by Christians and by Pagans.

If you use a tree, make a big deal out of it. Put it up in the afternoon of Yule and leave it up either for twelve days (one for each month, and also to tie in with medieval Twelfth Night customs) or until Imbolc (or until the needles start to fall off if you use a cut tree).

Whether to use a cut tree, live tree to be planted in the spring, or artificial tree is a personal decision. Pagans can use any in good conscience. A live tree is perhaps the best, but we don't all have the luxury of land to plant one on. Cut trees are grown on farms, and if it will be disposed of responsibly a Pagan should feel no worse about using one than about eating a carrot. Many communities collect trees for mulching or erosion control, or you could put yours in the woods where it will provide shelter for small animals. Pagans are not overly fond of plastic, but an artificial tree, which will last for years, is an entirely appropriate use for it. If a member of your family has allergies it may be your only choice.

Many commercially available or easily homemade tree decorations are fine for Yule trees. You can use small masks like the Romans, who hung masks of Bacchus on trees for Saturnalia, their Midwinter feast. Strung cranberries (solar symbols) and popcorn, which can be put outside for birds, are homey and traditional. Roosters, horses, golden balls and discs, candles, oranges, flame-colored ribbons and streamers, wheels, chariots, lights, wreaths, six-pointed stars, dragons, phoenixes, eagles, hawks, lions—all are sun symbols. Simple colored balls in the sun colors of red, gold, yellow, and orange are appropriate as well as figures of elves and fairies. And don't forget the symbols of winter—the white balls, icicles, and snowflakes.

A good meal for the afternoon (while trimming the tree) is a light one that leaves room for feasting later and doesn't take much time to make. Soup, salad, and melted cheese on bread is enough. For a special treat, toast pita bread (white or whole wheat) under the broiler, cover with sliced tomatoes, broil again, and then top with cheddar cheese sprinkled with chopped basil. Broil until the cheese melts. It's messy to eat, but good, and full of solar symbolism—round bread, golden cheese, and red wheels of tomato make up your own suns on earth.

For drinks, serve cranberry or orange juice or eggnog. Cranberry juice is good served hot, especially with clove and cinnamon added. For a simple mulled wine, add cloves and cinnamon sticks to sangria. Heat over low heat (do not boil) and serve. There will be more spice flavor if the spices are soaked in the wine overnight in the refrigerator before heating. For decoration and a little extra flavor, you can add an orange or lemon studded with cloves.

When the tree is set up in its stand and the decorations are ready to hang, gather around the tree with a bowl of water and an aspergill made of evergreen branches. An adult says:

> *The Spirit of Growth is here in our house,*
> *here in the midst of winter,*
> *to tell us to wait*
> *with hope and with longing*
> *for the Sun's return*
> *and green's rebirth.*

Then sprinkle the tree and each other, and decorate. You may turn on the lights momentarily to test them, but do not leave them on longer than necessary until after the night ritual.

The ritual extinguishing and relighting of fires is found in many traditions. The day on which it is done varies, but Yule is popular. Although we no longer have a central hearth with a continually burning fire many of us do have appliances with continually burning pilot lights that, though they lack romance, certainly serve the same function. These may be turned off early in the day (remember to turn off the gas as well!) and relit during the ritual. It will get cold. Real gung ho Pagans can try going without heat, hot water, or cooked food for the day.

Decorations: Candles, lights of all kinds, evergreens, roosters, suns, holly and ivy, mistletoe (the plant so Pagan it was banned from churches), and luminaria (paper bags filled partway with sand, that have a lit candle in the sand—the candle shines through with a golden brown glow, perfect for Yule).

Food and drink: Anything round, golden, or hot. Shortbread, fruitcake, eggnog, mulled wine, cranberry juice, orange juice, corn bread baked in a round pan, oranges, gingerbread, chicken, suet pudding (more commonly called "plum pudding," even though it has no plums in it). It is often served with brandy poured on it and lit, making it a burning wheel and thus a perfect symbol of Yule (although not originally Pagan). Here is my family's recipe:

3 cups flour
1 cup ground suet
1 cup raisins or currants
1 tsp. baking soda
1 tsp. cinnamon
$1/2$ tsp ground clove
$1/4$ tsp. nutmeg
1 tsp. salt
1 cup molasses
1 cup milk

Mix everything together and put in a greased round pan. Fill only half full. Cover tightly with foil and put on a rack in a large pot. Fill with water to halfway up the pan. Steam for three hours, adding water when necessary. When cool, remove from the pan, wrap in foil, and put in the refrigerator or freezer. This has to be made at least a month in advance to allow the flavors to mellow.

To reheat, steam again. It may also be steamed sliced, with the slices wrapped in foil. Serve with flaming brandy or hard sauce (butter with enough confectioners sugar to make it stiff; vanilla extract or brandy may also be added).

Traditions to raid: St. Lucy's Day (Swedish; December 13th), Hanukkah (Jewish; dates vary), Saturnalia (Roman; December 17th-24th), Kwanzaa (African-American; December 26th-January 1st).

After decorating the tree, but before lighting it (except for a quick check of the lights), eat your evening meal. Use your best dishes and have appropriate foods. These could be the foods listed above or culturally traditional Midwinter and festival foods.

After your meal, clear the table. Wash and dry the dishes and put them away. Then take every candle you own and put it in some kind of holder. Use saucers and bowls if you run out of candlesticks. Melt some wax onto the dish and stick the candle in it before the wax hardens. You might want to do this earlier in the day as it can take some time. Put all these candles on the table, with your sun candle in the middle. Turn off every light in the house. When the house is dark and everyone is seated, an adult says:

> *For half the year, day by day,*
> *slowly the world has grown darker.*
> *For half the year, night by night,*
> *slowly the dark has grown longer.*
> *Tonight that ends*
> *and the wheel turns.*
> *Our land turns back to the light.*

Light the sun candle.

> *The darkness was never complete*
> *A spark was always waiting*
> *to return and turn again.*
> *And now it will grow greater and greater.*
> *The light will come back.*

The cold will go away.
And once more we will dance in the warmth
until the wheel turns again.
It has always been this way
The wheel turning from darkness to light
and back again
and our people have always known this
and have turned with it.

All:

The wheel is turning
and light's returning.

An adult starts a litany. The response to each line is:

The light is reborn.

With each answer another candle is lit, until they are all burning. The lines of the litany can go like this:

In the greatest darkness
Out of Winter's cold
From our deepest fears
When we most despair
When all seems lost
When the earth lies waste
When animals hide
From fallen leaves
When the river is frozen
When the ground is hard
From the midst of the wasteland
When hope is gone
Out from the hard times.

Continue in this way until half the candles are lit. Then change the emphasis of the litany like this:

Shadows are fleeing
Light is returning
Warmth will come again

Summer will be here once more
Plants will grow again
Animals will be seen once more
Life will continue
Green will come again
Death will not be forever.

Continue until all the candles are lit. Then, take a deep breath, bask in the candlelight for just a second, and run through the house (carry small children) and turn on every light. Running is important to add a touch of festivity and abandon. Don't forget closets, attics, stoves, and even flashlights. If you have lights for decorations on a Yule tree or outside, turn them on as well. You will discover that children are quite good at finding lights you have forgotten.

When all the lights are on, return to the table. Sit in the glow for a while, eating, drinking, and talking. This is one of my favorite moments of the year; I can feel the light through the walls. For a family in which turning off unneeded lights is an obsession, this is a special moment indeed. The feeling stays with me for days.

Bring out the cookies and eggnog and have some fun. Then slowly go through the house again, turning the lights back off. Blow out the candles. Leave the sun candle burning until you have to go to bed. Light it first thing in the morning and leave it burning all day if you can. Burn it each day as long as the tree is up.

You may wish instead to celebrate at dawn. If you have adopted the Christian custom of presents under the tree, there is a good chance your children will be getting up at dawn anyway. Light the candles and house lights as soon as you see the sun. (Alternatively, you can start at false dawn, the period of growing light before the sun actually rises.) Because you will be present at the actual rebirth of the sun, dispense with the words for the lighting, or limit them to a simple:

The Sun is back
He is born again.

Then, with the lights still burning, you can open presents and eat breakfast.

It was (and I hope still is) traditional in some parts of England to bless the fruit trees at this time of year. People would make a bowl of wassail (a spiced ale beverage), drink some, and sprinkle the trees with some, crying out, "Waes-hail!" ("Be whole!") This was accompanied by loud noises, including the firing of guns.

To make wassail, heat (but do not boil) ale with ginger added. Use about half an inch of fresh ginger to each bottle of ale. When it is warm enough and the ale has picked up enough ginger flavor, sweeten to taste. While the ale is heating, core one apple for each bottle of ale and bake at 350° until soft. Add them to the ale when it is ready. Although children won't be able to drink the wassail, they can certainly shout, sprinkle, and make loud noises.

Imbolc

February 2nd has many names. Its Gaelic names are "Imbolc" (the "b" is silent) and Oimelc. The medieval Irish glossaries give the meaning as "ewe's milk." Modern scholars are not so sure, but propose "Imbolc" to be related to a word for bag, full belly, or womb. In English it is called "Candlemas" (a Christian name). An Anglo-Celtic name is "Brighid's Day." And to many Neo-Pagans it is "Lady's Day" (although some use that for Beltane or Ostara).

These many names show some of the meanings of the day. It is basically a precursor to spring. (In the gentle climate of Ireland, warmed by the Gulf Stream, it is considered the first day of spring.) Lambs are born; ewes lactate; candles are blessed; Brighid, Lady of Fire, returns; and the ground hog pokes his head out. In northern America, winter is half over, and households should therefore be no more than halfway through their winter stores of food and fuel.

The Gaelic sagas are silent about Imbolc's significance (it is not even mentioned in non-Gaelic Celtic traditions), but it is a day for which it is easy to find folk traditions. In America it is mostly known as "ground-hog day." The original idea was that if it was fair on Imbolc then winter would continue, but if it was foul, then winter was over. In Ireland the decision was made by the hedge-hog, an animal with many a role in folklore, but in America his place had to be taken by the ground hog. The traditions surrounding Brighid's Day in Ireland are extensive. (See page 116.)

From the Roman Lupercalia and the Christian Candlemas comes a theme of purification. The former took place on February

15th when a goat was sacrificed outside the city and two men, dressed only in thongs made from its hide, ran through Rome. They struck people as they went with thongs from the goatskin. It was especially fortunate for women to be struck. The Romans themselves didn't know the meaning of this ritual, but thought it had to do with fertility and purification in anticipation of the spring sowing. "Februa" appears to have a meaning connected with purification.

Candlemas, on the other hand, is a purely Christian feast. Hebrew religion required the ritual purification of women on a certain day after childbirth (a custom which survived into recent times as the churching of women). With the birth of Christ set on December 25th, the time for Mary's purification fell on February 2nd. The candle connection came from the words of Simeon in Luke 2:32, that Jesus would be "a light for revelation to the Gentiles," not from a Pagan source.

Some Pagan traditions have declared Imbolc to be the purification ("revirginization," if you will) of the Goddess after the birth of the sun god. This is great poetry and fine myth, but it must be remembered that it is a modern interpretation inspired by Christian practice rather than an ancient Pagan belief.

No matter the source, the purification theme is best suited to a Mediterranean climate, as a preparation for sowing. Pagans living in such a climate might wish to emphasize that theme. Those who live in a temperate climate would wish to emphasize the midpoint of winter.

Food: Dairy products, sprouts, fruitcakes (maybe you can finally finish that last bit of Yule fruitcake), lamb.

Traditions to raid: Candlemas (Christian; February 2nd), Lupercalia (Roman; February 15th), Valentine's Day (February 14th).

In New England we have something called "January Thaw." It's a period of a week or two when the temperature rises and some of the snow melts. When I was in high school my yard's snow was always the last on the street to melt in the spring. We would take advantage of January Thaw to shovel some of the snow onto the snow-warmed driveway and sidewalk, where it would melt, leaving that much less for the spring.

One peculiar thing about January Thaw is that it frequently came the first week of February. If your area has a similar weather event, consider celebrating Imbolc then, even if it actually comes in January.

Ritual of Melting

Prepare a collection of small bells (jingle bells will do fine), one set for each person. Go outside with them, a small candle (such as a birthday candle), matches, and an empty bowl. Draw a symbol of spring in the snow. This could be fire, a sun, a flower, running water, or anything else that means spring to you. Your children can help decide. They can each draw one of their own in a circle if you wish. Ring the bells to symbolize the melting of ice and snow, and say:

> *The snow will melt and Spring will come again.*

Put the candle in the middle of the symbol, light it, and say:

> *Here in the snow a spark of Spring is growing.*

Fill the bowl with snow and bring it inside, ringing the bells as you go. Leave the candle to burn out. Place the bowl on the table and have your holiday meal. At the end, an adult holds up the now-melted snow (it's OK to cheat a little and put it somewhere extra warm) and says:

> *The snow may lie deep.*

Everyone says:

> *But the melting time will come.*

The adult says:

> *The water may stand still in hard ice.*

Everyone says:

> *But the time will come for it to flow.*

While the bells are again rung, the adult then pours the water into another bowl, saying:

> See, it's true:
> Winter won't last forever!
> The sun is indeed growing strong
> and bringing back the warmth.
> The snow will melt
> and the earth grow green again.

The water may then be used to bless the family members or to water a plant.

Brighid's Day

Under the name of "Brighid's Day," Imbolc is a living festival in Ireland. The Irish of course have a strong history of blending the Old Ways with Catholicism, and in their Brighid's Day they have most likely preserved many customs from Pagan days.

The Irish goddess Brighid (or Brigid, Bride, or Brigit, traditionally pronounced "Breed," but now often pronounced like the name "Bridget"), who became the Catholic St. Bridget, is a multi-faceted (or multiple) goddess of poetry, smithing, healing, fire, and spring. Her name means "The High or Exalted One," and from this and from her functions it is obvious that she is a very great goddess. Her fire associations most likely came from the forge of the smith, the inspiration of the poet, and the life heat of the healer. (Then again, it may have been the other way around, and she may have been a fire goddess first.) In the folk tradition, from which this ritual comes, she has worn down some (as deities tend to do), and now her fire burns on the hearth of Irish homes, where she serves as the home guardian. She is thus a partial equivalent of Hestia or Vesta; she watches over all energy in a house and protects the house from danger, especially from fire.

Brighid is the patroness of all who work with cows, and all who deal in dairy products. She travels the world with her red-eared white cow, and is especially likely to come to visit on her day.

Offerings are left out for Brighid and her cow, which are taken by the poor in her name. This is therefore a traditional day for giving charity, especially food, and especially to the homeless.

If you celebrate this ritual, you will have called Brighid as your hearth guardian. If you have an affinity with a different hearth guardian, use her name and symbol in the ritual or perform a different ritual.

For the ritual you will need a Brighid's cross. This takes different forms in different parts of Ireland. The most common and simplest of these is essentially a god's eye made of two sticks and straw. However, the best-known (in this country at least) is an off-center cross. The legends of St. Bridget say she wove the first one while explaining Christianity to her father, but it is possibly pre-Christian. It is usually interpreted as a fire-wheel, which certainly describes its off-center version, but this description doesn't fit the other forms.

Figure 4. Brighid's Cross

Brighid's crosses may be bought in Irish craft stores. It is also customary to burn last year's, but the same one can be used year after year. It you can't find one, don't worry; making them is one of the traditional events of the day.

They may be made from reeds, straw, or construction paper. If you are using dry reeds or straw, soak the materials overnight to soften them. Some reeds will not soften much, so you may want to experiment by yourself before trying this with children. The pieces may be of any convenient length. The cross you will end up with will be slightly larger than the length of one piece.

To start, bend two pieces in their middles to form loops. (This will be done with each piece as you make the cross.) Link them together as shown in Figure 5a. Turn the pieces so they lie flat and form a right angle as in Figure 5b. This is the only time in the construction when the pieces will be hooked through each other like this. This two-piece construction is the base.

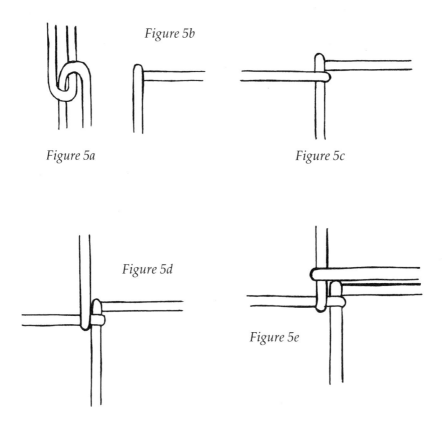

Figure 5b

Figure 5a

Figure 5c

Figure 5d

Figure 5e

Making Brighid's Cross

Next bend another piece and loop it over one of the two base pieces as shown in Figure 5c. Both legs of the loop in the new piece pass over both legs of the base piece. Pull it tight and hold it in place.

Bend another piece and loop it over the two legs of the last piece you put on (Figure 5d). Continue to do so as in Figure 5e until the cross is the size you want. Tie the ends together with string, reed, or straw (tape construction paper) and trim.

In old Ireland there was one hearth, over which to hang the cross. When more than one was made, they were hung other places as well. The hearth was the source of the household's warmth, cooking, light, and hot water. Modern houses have several different devices to do these things. Rather than have several crosses, one for each, the cross is hung over the stove and the others (furnace and water heater) make do with crosses drawn on them with charcoal. Indeed, in some parts of Ireland Brighid's crosses were drawn on people and walls with charcoal as a mark of protection. You may wish to do this as well. If you have several children and they each make one, you will have to hang all the crosses up, either together or one at each "hearth."

The crosses are said to protect the house from lightning, fire, and storm, and family members from illness.

Brighid's Day Ritual

Set the table with your best dishes. Prepare the food for the meal, but do not cook it yet.

Among the food include a loaf of bread in the shape of a Brighid's cross. Use your favorite bread recipe for this. After the last rising, divide the dough in fourths. Shape each piece into a long roll and fold in half. Hook the piece together to make a simple Brighid's cross and squeeze the tips together. You can bake it the day before or later in the ritual with the rest of the food.

When everything is ready, a woman or girl from the family goes outside with the cross and a lit candle. Alternatively, use a small oil lamp which you can keep next to the stove the rest of the year. She knocks on the door and says:

> Brighid is here, to bless this house.
> Open the door, and let her enter.

She does this three times. After the third time, those inside open the door and say:

> *Brighid, Brighid,*
> *Come in, come in:*
> *Welcome to our house.*
> *A thousand times welcome.*

Brighid comes in and holds up the candle and cross. The others say:

> *Lady of Fire,*
> *Burn in our hearts.*
> *Bring the Spring.*

She then passes the cross over the flame, saying:

> *May the blessing of Brighid be on this cross*
> *and on the place where it hangs*
> *and on all who see it*
> *through all the year.*

If the weather is too cold, instead of having a person outside, just put the cross outside, near the door. Put the candle or lamp next to it. When everyone is ready, welcome Brighid and open the door. Bring in the cross and candle and light the candle with the words beginning "Lady of Fire." Then continue with the ritual as written. This may also be done if there is no woman or girl to be Brighid.

One person takes the candle and another the cross and everyone goes to every room in the house. A child can carry the cross. If you have more than one child, they can take turns, changing when you go from one room to another. In each room the cross and candle are held up while someone says:

> *Brighid, Lady of Fire,*
> *Watch over this room.*

Mark Brighid's crosses with charcoal on your water heater, furnace, and fireplaces or woodstoves as you come to them.

You may wish to bring incense with you as well. Pine is an appropriate incense for Brighid, as it burns fast and hot. The needles of your Yule tree, if you use a cut one, are perfect.

Go to your kitchen last. If you have a gas stove, blow out the pilot light. Relight it with the flame of the candle (using something as an intermediary) while saying:

> *It is Brighid's fire that cooks our food.*

(If you relit your pilot light at Yule, do not do so now.)
Then hang the cross over the stove, saying:

> *Brighid, Queen of the Hearth,*
> *Keep us safe,*
> *Keep us warm,*
> *Extend your blessing over this our home.*

After the cross is hung turn on the oven to start cooking your food. Put the lit candle on the table until after the meal is over. While waiting for the food to cook, spend time doing something as a family.

After dinner the candle is put out by the one who was Brighid at the door (or by the mother or father if you didn't have someone at the door). She says:

> *Brighid will shine in our house*
> *though the whole year.*

Everyone says:

> *Blessings to our Lady Brighid.*

Each time you cook or bake, as you turn the oven on say:

> *I cook with Brighid's fire.*

This is a good reinforcement of her function as hearth guardian. If you use an oil lamp instead of a candle for the ritual, light it when you cook, especially on religious holidays.

Ostara

Imbolc brings the promise of new warmth and light. But it isn't until Ostara that the light is equal to the darkness. For Ostara is the Spring Equinox—the "equal night." After Ostara, there can be no doubt. The tide has definitely turned. The light half of the year has begun.

"Ostara" is one of a number of similar names that are used for this day. "Eoster" and "Eostre" are also popular, and, especially among Norse Pagans, "Easter." It is ironic that the English word for the holiest day in the Christian year should have a Pagan origin. Bede relates it to Eostre, the Germanic spring goddess. It definitely comes from the Indo-European "Ausro," from the root "aus," meaning "to rise." Johann Knobloch has theorized that the Germanic word therefore originally meant "dawn" (Robbins, 1978, p. 202). Ostara is the dawn of the year, then.

The choice among the different names is up to you. "Easter," while defensible, is confusing. "Ostara" is Old High German, but it fits Modern English better than the Old English "Eoster" and is probably the best choice. Some Pagans call it "Lady Day." This is one of the names of the Feast of the Annunciation (March 25th), and is probably of Christian origin.

One point that must be made here is that "Easter" is not related to "Ishtar" or "Astarte." The names of these goddesses are Semitic, not Indo-European. It is true, however, that their myths and rituals are sympathetic to Ostara, and may be incorporated into its celebration (subject to the removal of harvest associations).

Although its name is Germanic, the Pagan Germans didn't actually celebrate the Spring Equinox. It may have been celebrated in northern Europe in Neolithic times, but in the recorded period its first introduction there is by the Romans. The Celts didn't celebrate the equinoxes at all, so the next infusion into the north was by the Christians.

In southern Europe and the Ancient Near East things were different. Among many of the peoples there (the Romans and Babylonians, for instance) Ostara was New Year's. The Romans even originally had a gap between the end of December and the equinox which wasn't on the calendar (hence the names of October-December, the 8th-10th months of the year). When the equinox came around, the agricultural year started again.

As mentioned earlier, in the Ancient Near East the Spring Equinox was the time of the barley harvest. If you wish to include customs from that area in your Ostara celebration, then, be careful to distinguish which customs are appropriate to the equinox and which are appropriate to harvest.

Since the Celts didn't celebrate Ostara, there is some overlap between it and the Celtic festivals. Ostara can be seen as the culmination of Imbolc or as a precursor to Beltane; alternatively, the main emphasis can be on the solar or astrological significance of the day.

The Jewish holiday of Passover occurs about this time. While it has fewer Pagan elements than Easter, it owes its origins in part to the spring festivals of the ancient Near East. (I am not referring to the Exodus but to the way in which this event is celebrated.)

Because of the difference of seasons, though, Passover is not a good source of customs for Pagans. It originated at the beginning of the main grain harvest, when the winter rains gave way to summer showers. As celebrated today, Passover has few accretions from European Paganism. In fact, with its emphasis on the stories of the Jewish people and the place set for Elijah, it reminds me most of Samhain.

The secular customs that surround Easter are not exactly Christian, but they may not be specifically Pagan either. Eggs are obvious symbols of new life, and the flamboyant mating of rabbits and hares at this time ("mad as a March hare") make them equally appropriate. They are certainly found in many Pagan cultures. In fact, most secular Easter customs can be adopted wholeheartedly by Neo-Pagans. Some have been invented by Christians, but as natural reactions to the seasons rather than as developments of the Christian message.

So colored eggs, baskets, jelly beans, candy rabbits, and flowers—use them all. Chocolate bunnies may not be of Pagan origin, but who cares? They are festive and many people certainly view chocolate with religious fervor.

If you have a garden, this is a good day to plant it if you live in an area where the threat of frost has passed. If you live in a cold climate, start planting it in peat pots on this day, to be planted outside on May Day. When you plant your garden, leave part of it (or at least part of your yard) for the spirits of the wild. Give them offerings each year before planting. If you do not have a good relationship with the wild you have no business planting a garden.

If you don't think you have space for a garden, remember that a garden can be tomato plants on a balcony, peas on a sun porch, or herbs growing in a sunny window. It is important for Pagans to be involved in the production of at least part of their own food. It's an easy way to be involved in the life and death cycle.

Go fly a kite. It is March, after all, the month of wind. Make it a bright yellow one, with ribbons hanging from it, or one in the shape of a solar hawk or eagle.

Decorations: Suns, wind socks, leaves, new flowers (especially yellow ones such as daffodils or forsythias), pussy willows. The foliage can be used to bless, either by using them as aspergills or simply by passing them by family members. Anything yellow or green, especially spring green. Rabbits, eggs—all the secular Easter symbols are fine.

Food: Solar foods—chicken, red, yellow, and orange side dishes. Quiche is good, being round, golden, and made of eggs. To relieve the monotony, include a salad with strong green colors. Also include sprouts in it. Eggs.

Traditions to raid: St. Patrick's Day (March 17th), Easter, Spring Cleaning, April Fool's Day.

Use your best dishes. Put the sun candle in the center of the table, with early spring flowers around it if any are up yet.

In the first ritual, Ostara is a precursor of Beltane. Warmth is predicted and invoked, and the beginning of spring is acknowledged. The second ritual sees the fulfillment of Imbolc. Winter is over, and snow and ice are melting. Both rituals work with the solar symbolism that is the hallmark of the day.

Ritual 1

Prepare an outdoor fire, either a bonfire or in a barbecue. Gather around it in daylight with noisemakers. These can be drums (put right on the ground, even if frame drums), rattles, horns, and any of the little noisemakers sold for parties. The father has the sun candle and matches. He holds them up and says:

We are here to wake up the spring.

He then lights the candle and holds it up to the sun. Then, from it, he lights the fire (using intermediary tapers or matches), saying:

> *Here in front of us the fire leaps up,*
> *reaching from us up to the sky*
> *up to where the sun is shining*
> *the sun in the sky that is looking down*
> *looking down here where our fire is burning.*
> *Fire of the Sun,*
> *burn in our midst.*
> *Fire of the Sun,*
> *Burn in our midst.*
> *Fire of the Spring,*
> *Burn in our midst.*
> *Warm us and the world*
> *as the season turns to spring.*

Everyone joins in with "Burn in our midst."

Then everyone makes noise, using their noisemakers and pounding on the ground. While they do this, they repeat:

> *Wake up, Earth.*

Continue the noisemaking until you want to stop. If it is warm enough, you can stay outside around the fire. If not, go inside for a meal.

Ritual 2

Boil thirteen eggs sometime during the day. If there are a large number of people in your family, boil twenty-five. Dye all but one of them sun colors (red, yellow, and orange). This can be done the previous day if time is a problem. Leave one white. At dinner, put them in a bowl next to the sun candle in the middle of your table. Put the white egg on the top of the pile. What you will have is a bowl of one or two suns for each month of the year, plus one winter egg.

After sacred time is established, an adult picks up the white egg and bangs it on the table to crack it, and removes the shell, saying:

> *The ice cracks.*

He removes the white, saying:

The snow melts.

He holds up the yolk, saying:

The Sun is coming back.
And now that he is armed
and now that he is strong
He will chase away the cold
he will bring us spring
and summer is sure to follow.

Pass around the pieces of the egg for everyone to share before starting the rest of the meal. Eat the colored eggs with the meal. If desired, one can be reserved for an offering.

An Easter tradition practiced in many places that is good here (especially if your version of the Wheel of the Year puts the beginning of the battle between winter and spring at the Spring Equinox) is egg fights. Each person chooses an egg. Two people then face the small ends of their eggs towards each other. One of them hits the other's egg with his own. When one person's cracks, he turns his around and has another chance with the other side. When both ends of an egg are cracked, that person is out. The game continues until one egg is triumphant.

Another game that is fun to play is balancing eggs. There is a belief that the only day that a hardboiled egg can be balanced on end is the equinox. (Not true, unfortunately; it can be done any time, although it is always difficult.) The idea would seem to be that on the day of balance between night and day other things can be balanced too. Since you'll have a whole bowl of them in front of you it would be hard to keep from giving it a try.

Save the colored shells until May Day.

May Day

May Day, called "Beltane" ("Bright Fire") by the Gaels, is the great day of celebration in Europe, celebrated from Ireland to Russia. Finally the weather is warm. Winter is officially over. In Ireland, it was the day that the cattle were sent to their summer pastures.

Beltane is halfway around the year from Samhain, and they are similar in many ways. Both are days when the veil is thinnest between the worlds, both are bonfire days, both begin halves of the year. In Welsh legend, Beltane is the day for supernatural happenings, as Samhain is in Ireland.

In Scotland, Beltane once lasted for eight days, with the first and the last especially important. This makes it one more day than Samhain, perhaps to make the time celebrating life longer than that celebrating death.

Since Beltane got its name from its bonfires, it is a perfect day for one. (Beltane might also mean "Bel's Fire," Bel apparently being a solar god. His name survives in Latinized forms such as Belenus, and is similar but completely unrelated to the Semitic god Baal.) In the ritual, the bonfire has been replaced with a barbecue, but if you can have a bonfire, do so.

In Celtic times, cattle were driven between two bonfires on Beltane to protect them before they were sent out to pasture. People would jump over the fires, both as a blessing and for sheer fun or sport. (If you do this, please be careful. Don't wear loose fitting clothes, and don't push yourself to see who can jump the farthest or over the highest flames. It isn't a contest.) For a couple to jump over a Beltane fire together is as good as an announcement of betrothal. (Perhaps arranged while a-Maying in the woods the night before?)

This is a day that deserves our full celebration. Take the day off, take the kids out of school, and go on a picnic. Play outdoor games: throw around a ball, have a game of tag, run races, play croquet. Archery is particularly associated with this day, being found in both England (where of course it was connected with Robin Hood) and Germany. All target games are good.

May Day as we know it is a combination of the Celtic Beltane, with its bonfires and rowan, and the Roman Floralia, with its May Queen and flowers. The Floralia elements have come to predominate, as shown by what Leach (pp. 695-6) lists as elements of a typical European May Day celebration:

1. Gathering of green branches and flowers on May Eve or very early May Day morning.

2. Choosing and crowning a May Queen (often also a King) who goes singing from door to door carrying flowers or a May Tree, soliciting donations in return for the "blessing of the May." She was seen by the English as representing the Roman goddess Flora.

3. Erection and decoration of a Maypole, Tree, or Bush.

Pick a tree or bush in your yard and hang it with ribbons, flowers, and the eggshells saved from Ostara. This is the May Bush, around which May rituals are frequently performed. Maypoles are better suited for gatherings larger than a family. If you like, you can see the May Bush as the family version of the Maypole. It is customary to dance around it, just as the Maypole is danced around.

Large indoor plants such as ficus trees can be used as May Bushes. Ribbons can also decorate decks, balconies, or windows. Our garden each summer is decorated with ribbons in the colors of the elements. We buy new ribbons each year, and the old ones are added to the supply for next spring's May Day.

Leave cloths out on the eve to soak up the dew. This dew can then used for a variety of purposes. Washing with it is said to make the skin beautiful, and it is a good basis for herbal brews.

Oddly enough, there is a Roman holiday that is even more similar to Beltane than Floralia is. On April 21st, the Romans celebrated Parilia. For this shepherd's festival, the animals' stalls were swept, and decorated with foliage. Offerings of cakes, milk, and meat were offered to Pales, a pastoral deity. (The Romans did not know whether Pales was a god or a goddess.) The flocks were then driven through fires and blessed with the smoke, after which the people washed their hands in dew, drank milk and wine, and jumped three times over the fires to the east.

The intent of Parilia was to increase the fertility and milk production of the herds. What make this festival particularly interesting is the date. Since the climate in Rome is milder than in the

British Isles, it is only to be expected that the Romans would celebrate the same festival earlier than the Celts. And here it is—flocks driven through bonfires and people purified in dew. This is a clear example of a widespread celebration of this season.

If your children are older, and especially if there are other Pagans in the area, they should either get up very early or stay up very late to gather greens to decorate each others' doors. The rowan is the traditional source of decorations, although any greenery and flowers will do. The deed should be done in time to be discovered by the sun.

The eve of May Day is Winter's last hurrah. One last night of rule, and then he dies. Six months ago the figure of Winter was made and feted; now do it once more. Drink toasts to him and offer to him.

Decorations: Flowers, ribbons, rowan branches, branches with new leaves or buds, wreaths of flowers. Decorate your shrine with flowers.

Food and drink: May wine (sweet wine flavored with woodruff; it can be bought already prepared), especially with strawberry halves in the glasses, green food (especially fresh mint), violets (both the flowers and the leaves can be eaten, and the flowers look interesting in a salad).

Traditions to raid: Parilia (April 21st), Floralia (Roman; April 28th-May 3rd).

Ritual

May Day, the great day of picnics, is a perfect day for a barbecue. Prepare the grill. If this is you first barbecue of the season, remove all the ashes from last year and start a new season. Be sure to use lots of lighter fluid. You want it to blaze up. Practice conservation some other time; May Day is all about excess.

The parts of the father may be performed instead by the oldest male present (provided he has come of age). The parts assigned to the May Queen may be performed by any of the women present. Which one does so is chosen by lot. Use marbles in a box, with one of a different color, or roll dice or draw cards. (The first May Day after a woman comes of age, she is automatically entitled to preside.) The woman chosen is the May Queen and should be crowned with a wreath of flowers or leaves before the ritual.

Put matches, lighter fluid, the figure of Winter, a pot (either a cauldron that you use in coven or personal rituals, or one you use for cooking), and a bucket or pot of water (for fire safety) next to the barbecue. When everything is ready, gather about the barbecue. The May Queen says:

> *The fire of spring has been burning.*
> *The Wheel of the Year has been turning.*
> *The fire and the wheel have brought us here*
> *to May Day, beginning of summer.*
> *It's time now to light the fire of summer*
> *and to burn away all that remains of winter.*

Then the father lights the barbecue. (Give it one more squirt of lighter fluid first.) When the flames have died down some, the May Queen takes the figure of Winter and lights it. She puts it into the pot or cauldron to finish burning. If your backyard is private enough or the neighbors sufficiently understanding, do the burning (or perhaps the whole ritual) in the garden itself. While Winter burns, say:

> *Winter is gone and summer is here.*
> *Winter is dead and summer is alive.*
> *Winter is ashes in summer's green earth.*

Fan the smoke so it blows on each person present as a blessing. When Winter is all burnt, scatter the ashes in the garden. Dig a deep hole earlier in the day to put the remains in, in case Winter doesn't burn completely. (If you have made him out of dead grass this is more likely than if he is made of garden plants.) If you don't have a garden, the ashes can be scattered in a local wild spot or a friend's garden. As you bury or scatter them say:

> *From the ashes of winter*
> *Summer springs up:*
> *Green and bright and shining and warm.*

Throughout the year save nail clippings and hair trimmings (including stubble cleaned from electric razors) in a bag. After scattering the ashes, scatter the hair and nails and work them into the soil, saying:

> *From the Earth to us*
> *From us to the Earth*
> *The wheel is always turning.*

Then barbecue. Spare ribs are particularly good; the sacred pig, bright red, spicy (hot), and messy—perfect for a celebration.

The day after May Day transplant your peat pots and prepare the rest of the garden.

Midsummers

Midsummers, the Summer Solstice, is the high point of the sun. At no other time will it rise so far in the north or be so high at noon. What started at Yule reaches its completion.

The European traditions universally used bonfires and commonly water as well in their Midsummers celebrations. Wheels covered in straw were lit on fire and then rolled down hills to land in a pond, or were thrown straightaway into water. Bonfires were lit on hilltops. St. John's Day (June 23rd) is celebrated with bonfires in many places to this day, especially in Ireland.

Midsummers falls on the cusp of Cancer, a prime water sign, and Leo, a prime fire sign. This may explain the fire/water connection (although it is doubtful that German peasants were sufficiently versed in astrology to make this connection). Or maybe it's the direct opposition of fire and water that makes them attractive for a day such as this. Although it is the day on which the sun is the strongest, it is also the day on which it starts to weaken. Then again, perhaps the purpose is not so much to celebrate the sun's height as to mitigate its heat. The intent may well be to prevent drought during a crucial growing season by subordinating the sun wheel to water.

Midsummers calls for a bonfire if possible. If not, the barbecue can substitute. A good time for the barbecue ritual is noon, the high point of the sun, but a bonfire should be lit at sunset so it will show up better in the dark.

To include water in your celebrations while having fun with children, try water sports. These can be swimming, running through sprinklers, or water fights. It's hard to beat the fun and symbolism of sun-colored water balloons. This is a good day to establish a tradition of going to the beach.

The first two rituals use an aspergill. One way to make this is to tie a bunch of St. Johnswort (so called because it blooms about this day) together with a gold ribbon. After the ritual, hang the aspergill in your home. They are said to protect the house from lightning. If St. Johnswort does not bloom around this day in your area, use a flower that does, preferably a red or yellow one, or daisies ("day's eyes").

Decorations: Floating candles on a pool, a bird bath, or even in a basin. Suns.

Food: Summery food, food that is red or yellow, picnic food. Strawberries, watermelon, barbecued anything (but especially chicken and pork). Spicy food (Mexican food, with its golden corn and red tomatoes, is good).

Traditions to raid: John the Baptist's Day (June 23rd), July Fourth, Holi (Hindu spring festival).

Ritual 1

Once again the barbecue serves as a substitute bonfire. Pour the charcoal and soak it with lighter fluid. Put the grate on and on top of it a pot of water (you can use the same pot you used for May Day, but be careful of plastic handles. They can melt). Nearby put the lighter fluid, the matches, and an aspergill.

When everything is ready and everybody around the barbecue, establish sacred time. Then the father (or the oldest male present) says:

> *Today the wheel has come to a special point.*
> *Since Yule the light has been growing.*
> *At Ostara the light became greater than the dark*
> *and it kept on growing.*
> *It has grown until today:*
> *Midsummers,*
> *The middle of the light time.*
> *Tomorrow the light will start to fade*
> *as the wheel turns to darkness*
> *until it is Yule again.*

But today it is bright
Today the sun is high
Today the world is warm and bright
and we celebrate this with fire.
The Lord Sun blazes above
Our fire blazes below.

He lights the fire (with one more squirt of lighter fluid first). When the flames have died down a bit, everyone can take an aspergill, dip it in the water, and sprinkle everyone else with it. Then take the pot off and, after it cools, water your garden or a tree with it. While waiting for the coals to be ready, a water fight would be a good idea. Then barbecue.

Ritual 2

This one is written to be performed on a beach. If you are lucky enough to live near the ocean that would be perfect. If not, a lake or pond is fine. It can be (and has been) performed quite satisfactorily inside with a bowl of water. Start it at noon.

You will need a bucket or basin (a sand pail works fine), a candle, something to sprinkle water with, and matches. Go down to the water and fill the bucket. Bring it back up the beach. Somewhere in between the high and low tide marks is best. That is the in-between area, neither land nor water, and thus sacred. Light the candle and hold it up and say:

The sun is high
on the longest day.

Lower it to the surface of the water and say:

Starting today it starts to get darker
as the sun goes into the water.

Submerge the candle and say:

The sun goes into the water
blesses it,
and fertilizes it.

Use the water to sprinkle to the four quarters, saying:

The waters of life flow to all directions of the Earth.

Sprinkle each other, saying:

And they bless all who live on it.

Follow the ritual with a water fight, swimming, a picnic, and other beach activities. If you do it at home, play throwing games, with balls and throwing disks, or water games (squirt guns, sprinklers, and water balloons).

Ritual 3

If you are fortunate enough to have a home where you can have a bonfire, that is the best way to celebrate Midsummers. Make it big and of very dry wood. Use lots of tinder and don't rule out aids such as lighter fluid. Use a torch to light it. Your pile should light quickly and impressively. Remember to have water or a fire extinguisher nearby in case the fire gets out of hand.

Use the same firelighting ritual as Ritual 1. As the flames start to rise up, the father says:

The Sun high in the sky
The Sun here on earth.

The others can repeat this, perhaps to drumming or other instruments. Sing, dance, tell stories, toast marshmallows. It can be jumped over, like the May Day fire (with the same caution). Small children can be carried over when it has died down very low.

The Midsummers fire is the time to destroy broken or worn religious objects. These must be disposed of in a respectful way, and although some might be buried or cast into the sea, burning is best for those that can be burnt.

Don't leave the fire before it is all out and the ashes cold. The ashes can be used in blessings. Put them on your garden and on your threshold, or draw protective symbols (see Appendix) with them on your house and each other.

Lammas

Lammas begins the harvest season. It is the feast of first fruits, the first of the three harvest festivals. Grain is ripening, and the first apples are ready. Although the traditional date is August 1st, if you farm and have a major crop, celebrate Lammas (under the name "Feast of First Fruits") when that crop becomes ripe and then again on the traditional date in honor of the grain. If your major crop is grain, celebrate it once when the grain starts to be ready to harvest.

Lammas derives its name from the Old English "Hlafmas," or "Loaf-mass." The name says it all. It is the feast of bread. On this day in early Christian times (and the name is apparently Christian, although the traditions it reflects are probably Pagan) loaves made from the first grain were blessed in the church. In Pagan times, they were almost certainly used in some ritual. Perhaps they were blessed and shared. Perhaps they were given as offerings to the gods. First fruit offerings are nearly universal—the first of anything belongs to the gods.

In Ireland it was considered "just not done" to harvest grain any earlier than this; it was a sign that the previous year's harvest had not lasted long enough. This was a serious failing, either on the part of the farmer for not growing enough or on the part of his wife for not conserving the store. But the first grain was cut this morning and made into bread or porridge by evening.

The Gaelic word for this day is "Lughnasadh," pronounced "Loo-nah-sah"—the feast of Lugh. Lugh is a Celtic god, the one whose name is most widespread, from Lyons to Carlisle (which the Romans called "Luguvalium," "Strong in Lugh"). In Wales he was "Lleu Llaw Gyffes," "Lleu of the Skillful Hand," and in Ireland he was "Lugh Samhildanach" (pronounced "Loo Saw-vil-dah-nakh"), "Lugh, Skilled in all the Arts." "Lugh" and "Lleu" themselves mean "bright, shining," which has led some to describe him as a solar god, which he probably was not.

His titles describe him: he is the skillful one, the craftsman god. There is a wonderful story in the tale of the Battle of Magh Tuiredh of how Lugh came to the court at Tara while a feast was going on. It was the custom there for no one to be admitted during a feast unless he possessed a skill that no one who was already there possessed. Lugh listed his skills one by one—wright, smith, champion, harper, hero, poet, magician, healer, cupbearer, craftsman—and the door-keeper told him each time that there was already someone at Tara who could do that. Finally, Lugh asked if there was anyone who had all these skills. There was no one, and he was allowed to enter.

This is the Lugh we know from the tales, the god of skills and crafts, the shining ruler with the great spear. The date of his festival makes it possible that he was an agricultural deity identified with the ripening grain (perhaps identified with the shining spears of wheat?), but the myths do not seem to reflect this.

There seem to be two themes for this date, then. One is the agricultural, represented by the Saxon Lammas, and the other is the feast of Lugh, represented by the Irish Lughnasadh. Their common ground may be found in the blessing of agricultural tools before harvest. Unless you are a grower of grain this is not very meaningful, though. There are two rituals given here, one for Lammas, and one for Lughnasadh.

Lammas begins a strange time of the year. To most people it is high summer. These are the hottest days of the year. It is a time for vacations and the beach.

But look more closely. Wheat is ripening. Pokeberries appear. And what is that about the light of late afternoon? Not only is it fading earlier each day; there is something in it that whispers "fall." Its angle is changing, and shadows are growing. No, it isn't time to turn toward the dark yet, not by any means. But we can feel the shadow behind us, hard on our heels. Soon the days will be cold and dark. That is why the bread at each of the harvest festivals grows progressively darker.

For now, though, we celebrate this strange time—the Loaf Mass, the Feast of Lugh. The sun is high, the days are long and hot. The wheat is golden, ready to be cut. And we reflect on the coming harvest of all that we have done.

Decorations: Sickles, scythes, garden vegetables, corn dollies, grain, grapes, vines, poppies, dried grains.

Food: Early harvest foods, especially those grown in your area. Grain products, corn on the cob, grapes, plums. Sometimes the early apples are available for Lammas. If so, be sure to include them.

Traditions to raid: Feast of the Green Corn (Native American), Succoth (Jewish; dates vary).

Lammas Ritual

This is a time for the giving of your gains. Sometime during the harvest, between now and Samhain, give your major charity donation. Also leave out grain and bread for the wild animals in your area (even if these are just pigeons and sparrows).

Set the table with your best settings. Prepare all the food except that which will come from your own garden. This is the time for all harvests to be celebrated, so include anything you have produced since last Lammas—art, writing, crafts, music, money; any symbol of your work.

If you have a garden or farm, start the ritual there. In fact, if you have enough space and privacy, hold the entire ritual there, on a picnic table or even on the ground. If you do not grow food, include some grown in the local area, especially the early apples. Most areas have farms where you can pick your own produce. Take your children to them and they will see that food is not grown in supermarkets.

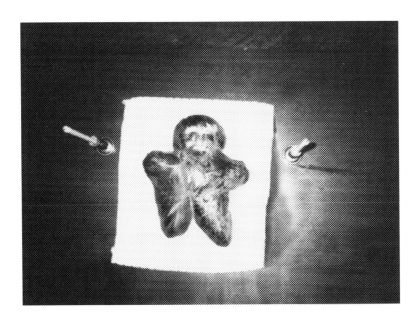

Lammas Bread

Bake a white bread in the shape of a man. The simplest way to do this is to take the dough after it has finished its last rise and cut three slits in it. (See Figure 6a.) Spread the two which are opposite each other out to form arms and spread the two bottom pieces apart to form legs (Figure 6b). Round out the head part and bake.

Figure 6a   *Figure 6b*

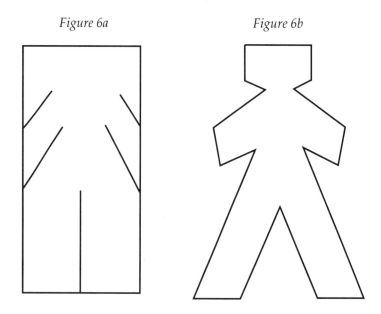

Making Lammas Bread

This bread will serve as the emblem of the God who has been given birth to by the Earth Mother and whose seeds now stand in the field. Some of these seeds will be eaten, and some will be used to impregnate the Earth again in the spring.

When the table is set and the food ready, with the bread as the centerpiece, go out to your garden. The father holds a sickle. While everybody harvests something, the father says:

> *Harvest is beginning*
> *Gold Sun, bright days,*
> *Gold wheat, bright bread.*

He uses the sickle to harvest something himself. (If you do not have a garden, these words can be said indoors.)

Then go in and gather around your table. The father lifts up the bread, holding the sickle in his other hand. He turns slowly around, presenting them to all directions, and then says:

> *Harvest is beginning,*
> *now in the height of summer.*
> *Cold will have its turn.*
> *But today it is warm.*
> *It is the feast of bright bread.*
> *The feast of first fruits.*
> *The hot time of the year*
> *while cold waits to creep in.*
> *Watch for the signs of fall:*
> *The fruits*
> *The berries*
> *The seeds*
> *They are coming.*
> *Soon the nights will be cold*
> *but now the days are hot.*

He holds the bread out to the mother, who holds her hands over it and says:

> *Our God is here, in the bread we eat.*

The father puts down the sickle and passes the bread around. Each person touches it in blessing and says:

> *We bless the bread,*
> *the bread blesses us.*

When the bread returns to the father, he blesses it and says:

> *We have all blessed the bread*
> *and now it will bless us.*

He cuts the head from the bread with the sickle and passes the bread around again. (He reserves the head.) This time everyone breaks off a piece of it. When everyone has a piece, all say:

The grain dies
and we eat it and live.
It blesses us
and we thank it.

Everyone eats a bit of it and the rest is served with the dinner. Any bread left over is left out as an offering. The head is either used as an offering or buried in the garden.

Lughnasadh Ritual

Gather together your tools—tool box, computer, pencils, pots and pans, brooms—whatever you use in your work. Use part or a symbol if the whole is too awkward. For example, if you don't want to carry a computer home from work, a photograph or a floppy disk can be used.

Children should include their own tools. School age children can use their school supplies. If a child is starting school in the fall, this is a wonderful time to have the supplies ready so they can be blessed. Younger children can use favorite toys; the proper work of young children is playing. Those old enough to have assigned chores can present the tools they use in those chores.

Put them together on a table in the room where you eat (not on the table you will be eating on, or there won't be room for the food). In the middle of the tools put a candle with matches next to it.

Wear the clothes you wear when you work with these tools.

After the food is prepared and the table set with your best settings, stand around the table with the tools on it. Establish sacred time. An adult lights the candle, saying:

Be with us, Lugh Samhildanach,
gifted in all the arts,
the holder and giver of all skills.
You who are open handed,
Be here today to give us your blessing.

Each person then holds his hands over his own tools and says (either individually or together):

I bless these tools in Lugh's name.
I will use them well and properly
in the service of the Gods and my people.

Then have your meal and talk about what work you have
done and what still remains to do.

Harvest

Fall is a uniquely ambivalent season. It is happy because it is the
harvest. In the old times it would be a season when there was lots of
food. Lots of work, but lots of food. Here in New England it is especially beautiful, and the air has a quality to it that defies description.

But fall is a time of death. Those beautiful leaves are being
stripped from the trees by the cold wind of the north and falling to
the ground to rot. The plants in the fields have made their seeds
and their work is done, so they grow brown and brittle. And the
first hard frost runs its sickle through the tomatoes.

It is only fitting that there be this ambivalence. After all, it is
the equinox, the time of balance. It is a crossover point, when what
came before and what is coming after are equally present. Harvest
is one of the four solar festivals, and its message is that light and
dark are in balance, though the dark may start to prevail. But we
know that halfway around the year is Ostara, Harvest's twin, and
only a few months away is Yule, the rebirth of light. From this
knowledge we gain the assurance to accept and even celebrate the
wonderful death of the year.

The first ritual is mostly a Harvest celebration and may appeal
more to those who don't want the thoughts of death to intrude too
strongly into this time of year. In the second the emphasis on the
dying of the year is stronger.

Both rituals are written to be done indoors. If it is warm and
you have a farm or a large garden they may be done there. This is
a day when instead of dressing up you might wish to dress down,
wearing the clothes you would wear to work in your garden.

The most important element of Harvest is the feast. Feasting,
especially at harvest time, is a religious act. Eating large amounts of
food in the company of family and friends is a way of thanking the

Earth, of cementing ties of love, and of reflecting the generosity of the season. Celebrate Harvest as an early Thanksgiving. (There is no Pagan reason not to celebrate the legal date as well.) Even if you do nothing else for this day, have a large festive meal. If preparation time is a problem the celebration may be shifted to a weekend.

For a meal to function as the centerpiece of a celebration, there must be special aspects to it. Particular foods eaten only on a holiday are obvious examples. Usually these are time-consuming to make, very tasty, and not particularly good for you.

A large number of people is another essential element to a feast. This is a time to invite friends and family, as many as you can handle, and as many as you think can handle helping you celebrate the day. On holidays it is especially good luck to be able to extend hospitality to a stranger (perhaps a friend of a friend).

Include with the meal whole wheat bread. Any whole wheat recipe will do. You can add sunflower seeds to it if you wish. Bake it in the shape of a sun. To do this, after the dough's final rising divide it into two pieces, one three times the size of the other. Shape the smaller piece into a round loaf. Roll the other into a long cylinder and then flatten it slightly. Cut it in a zigzag shape to make triangles. Although six is a traditional solar number, make more than that or your sun will look like a turtle. (Trust me on this one.)

Harvest Bread

Attach the triangles to the loaf (use an egg and water mixture to stick them on) to form the rays. Then bake it. Another way to avoid a whole wheat turtle is to shape the bread into a circle and cut a sun into it immediately before putting the bread in the oven.

Decorations: Sunflower seeds. Seeds in general. (They can be glued on paper or cardboard to make collages.) Sickles, scythes. Suns, autumn leaves. Fall decorations in general.

Food and drink: Seeds and foods made from seeds, foods that keep for the winter (roots and squashes), apples, goose, cider.

Traditions to raid: Succoth (Jewish; dates vary), Michaelmas (September 29th).

Ritual 1

At one end of your table put a bunch of dried ears of corn and some-thing harvested from your garden. Put the sun candle in the center with the bread next to it. When all the food is ready and the table set with your best dishes, establish sacred time. Then an adult says:

> *Today the wheel has come to a special point.*
> *For half the year now*
> *there has been more light than dark.*
> *Since Midsummers, though, the light*
> *   has been fading*
> *and today dark and light are equal*
> *and tomorrow the dark half of the year will begin.*
> *That is why we celebrate today.*
> *It is the balance point between light and dark.*
> *It is the beginning of the return of cold and dark.*
> *To the light time as it leaves we say:*
> *Hail and farewell!*

Light the sun candle and then continue:

> *To the dark time as it comes in we say Welcome!*
> *Be gentle with your cold, be loving in your dark.*

Hold up the bread, the corn, and some of the harvest, and say:

All summer the food has been growing
and now Harvest is here.
These are both sacred grains:
Corn, the sacred grain of this country
Wheat, the sacred grain of our ancestors.
We bless them.
May they bless us.

Pass the bread around, each person taking a piece and eating some. Then eat your meal. Afterwards, hang the corn on your front door, saying:

Hang here till Samhain comes
and the world grows darker still.
Hang here and bless our house
and all our coming in
and all our going out.

You may actually want to leave them there at least until Thanksgiving, the Harvest Home of American culture. In fact, the first, solar part of the ritual can be celebrated on the equinox and the second, harvest part on Thanksgiving.

Save part of the bread for offerings to your household guardians and also for the spirits of the wild.

Ritual 2

On the table put your best dishes, the sun candle, the sun bread, matches, some dried leaves, and a pot. Leave an outside door open. When the food is ready to serve and everyone at the table, establish sacred time. Then an adult gets up and slams the door shut and says:

Outdoors time is over
Indoors time begins.
More and more, now,
We will be pulling ourselves in.

Another adult lights the sun candle, saying:

He is in our midst,
the lord of the sky.

That person then picks up the dried leaves, lights them from the candle, and burns them in the pot, saying:

> *The Sun leaps up*
> *The Sun dies down*
> *It fades*
> *It passes*
> *and darkness comes*
> *but with one last flash of light.*

(This will make a lot of smoke. If this bothers you, do it outside at the beginning of the ritual, and then come inside, slamming the door on the way in.)

Then she takes the ashes and puts a mark on the faces and hands of everyone, saying:

> *In a flash of fire the autumn leaves burn*
> *and leave behind the ashes of winter.*

The marks are left on until the end of the meal, when they are wiped off with a wet cloth. The one doing the wiping says:

> *The rains of spring will come again*
> *and bring life from the ashes.*

After the meal at the end of either ritual, blow out the sun candle, saying:

> *The sun has gone into the fruits of summer*
> *and now it fades from the sky.*

8

The Times of the Moon

One reason Paganism has caught the imagination of so many people is its recognition of the female side of divinity. Although on the abstract theological level the Judeo-Christian God most of us grew up with is beyond gender, in His everyday manifestations He has been exclusively male. And now a religion comes along that claims that the divine is at least equally female. The concept has been transformative for many women and not a few men.

Neo-Pagans revere a multitude of female deities, but most have a special reverence for the Mother of All. She is just what her name says; the mother of phenomena, living or not, and mother in all its meanings. She is the giver of birth, the nourisher, the teacher, and the one who disciplines. Many Neo-Pagans see the other goddesses worshiped throughout the world as her different faces, and so she is simply called "the Goddess."

Although "Mother Earth" is one of her most common titles, the moon is equally her symbol, and Pagans give it special reverence. She shines down on everyone in the world, always changing, always the same. Even when she cannot be seen her presence is felt.

Even when apparently gone she sends us blessings and teaching. As Queen of the Night, she is the guardian of secrets. Because of the connection between the lengths of the menstrual cycle and the lunar cycle she is the patroness of women's mysteries. She rules the seas and our bodies in the tides. And her affect on lovers is well known.

As she changes above, the moon shows us the different faces of the Goddess. When the moon is waxing, she is the Maiden. She is the young and developing woman, the dancer and singer. When the moon is full, she is the Mother. It is she who holds us safe in her arms, and on whom we can call for help. And when she is dark, she is the Crone. She is the wise woman who teaches us her wisdom; she holds nothing back if we have the strength to learn it, but it is she who will call us to her in the end.

The moon taught people to measure time. Day and night are a flickering of light, and the year passes slowly, but the moon is our clock in the sky. The word "month" obviously is related to "moon," and the roots of words for measurement, though not related, are similar. The earliest measurements discovered were scratches on bone and stone that may have recorded the moon's phases.

It is the dark moon and the full moon that are most commonly celebrated by Neo-Pagans, the opposing points of Mother and Crone, the cusps on which the changes take place. The return of the moon is also a fitting day for celebration. She has not died, she has been changed, and life goes on. Indeed, this is a monthly reminder that life continues, even after seeming death.

It is for this reason some say it was the moon's cycle that taught us about rebirth. Certainly it holds deep mysteries: of change without death, of growth, of womanhood. Knowledge of these comes with maturity and practice. They are taught in covens and women's lodges, and are granted to those who meditate on the moon. In their fullness they are not dealt with easily in a family context.

But very young children can follow the moon's phases. They can be taught their names, shapes, and times of rising. They can also add to this knowledge with ritual awareness.

The mysteries of the changing of the moon will come to children in time. They are taught by myth, example, and experience. The family ritual, though, should be less heavy-handed. It is enough to observe three of the moon's points: the dark, the return, and the full. Time and the Goddess will do the rest.

Since the Bible forbids kissing one's hand to the moon (Job 31:26-7) it's a pretty good bet this was a Pagan custom. Form the horned hand (see Figure 7) with your main hand, by making a fist and extending your index and little fingers. Kiss it, and then extend your arm towards the moon so you can see the moon cradled between the horns. Greet the moon this way each night when you see her for the first time, especially on the new moon.

Figure 7. The Horned Hand

Decorations: Mirrors, crystals, white and silver ribbons. Or make a moon hanging: braid three ribbons or cords together. Use white, silver, and light blue, or white, light blue, and dark blue, or white, red, and black. These last three are used by some Pagans to symbolize the three phases of the moon. Braid only part of it and leave the rest hanging. Attach the braided end to the back of a round mirror, a silver metal disk, or a wooden disk painted silver, and hang it on the wall.

These rituals require a moon candle. This is a large white candle, preferably unscented. Keep it in your shrine. On moon festivals put it on the table. Its base may be decorated. Designs may be cut into it with a hot knife.

The Full Moon

The full moon comes about every four weeks. The exact time is given in almanacs and on many calendars. Be careful to know the proper night. For example, if the moon is full on Tuesday at 3:30 AM, the night of the full moon is Monday. Calendars will frequently give the day as Tuesday, so you have to know the time as well as the day.

Because the full moon comes often, it is best to have a variety of prayers for it. The outline of the ritual can stay the same from month to month, while the parts change. The unchanging element is the lighting of the moon candle and its blessing, followed by a prayer.

Use your best dishes and prepare a meal of lunar food (almonds, cucumbers, seafood [especially shellfish or crustaceans], croissants, pita bread, white wine, milk, honey, water). Make a batch of mooncakes. These can be just about any kind of light colored cookie, although almond is a traditional flavoring. Here's one recipe:

$1/4$ cup shortening
$1/4$ cup butter
$3/4$ cup sugar
1 oz. milk
$1/2$ tsp. vanilla
$1/2$ tsp. almond extract
2 cups flour
1 $1/2$ tsp. baking powder

Cream the first three ingredients. Add the remaining ingredients and blend with a wooden spoon. Roll $1/8$ inch thick on floured board and cut. Use a round cookie cutter. A small glass does a good job. Use the cutter to mark a crescent on them. Bake 8-9 minutes on ungreased cookie sheets in a 350° oven. Remove from the cookie sheets promptly and cool.

Adult women present should wear moon crowns. Since this is a mark of the identification between women and the moon, at least in part through their monthly cycles, girls should not wear them until they have come of age. Beautiful crowns made of silver or copper may be bought in occult shops, or one can be made from cloth. Cut two pieces of white felt in the shape shown in Figure 8a.

Figure 8a

Figure 8b   *Figure 8c*

Making the Moon Crown

On one, outline the moon shapes with silver liquid embroidery. (See Figure 8b.) Cut two small vertical slits in the middle of the other about half an inch apart. These may be reinforced with glue. After the glue is dry, thread a long blue or silver ribbon through them. (See Figure 8c.) It should be long enough to be tied around the head with plenty left over to hang down the back. Even out the ends of the ribbon and glue the two felt pieces together.

Ritual

Put your moon candle in the middle of the table in a bowl, preferably of clear or blue glass, filled with water. Use your best dishes. When the meal is ready, establish sacred time and say a mealtime prayer. (See Chapter 6.) Then one child says:

Why is tonight special?

An adult answers:

> *Tonight is the Full Moon.*

The child (or another one) says:

> *Why is that a special time?*

An adult answers:

> *The Full Moon is the Mother Time,*
> *time to be with family and friends,*
> *to celebrate all the wonderful things*
> *the Earth gives birth to.*

Or:

> *The Full Moon is our Mother*
> *Who wraps Her arms around us.*
> *She guards us and loves us*
> *and tonight we return that love.*

Another way to do this is for the adults to ask the children the questions and let them answer in their own words. As they grow, their understanding of the day will change and there will be a regular opportunity to express it.

The mother then lights the moon candle. She holds it above the table and everyone says:

> *The Goddess is shining, high in the sky.*

She returns it to the bowl of water and everyone says:

> *The Goddess is shining, here in our home.*

Everyone crosses their hands on their breasts and says:

> *The Goddess is shining, deep in our hearts.*

Then have your dinner. At the end, clear away the dinner things. Leave your glasses and the moon candle. Set the table again with cakes and drinks. Then an adult says:

> *We share the gifts of the Goddess with her*
> > *and each other*
> *on the night when she rides high in the sky.*

Pass the cakes around. While you do, one parent says:

> *Mother of us all,*
> *Watch over us.*
> *Hug us*
> *Hold us*
> *Wrap us round with your loving arms*
> *and keep us safe until the Moon is full again.*

After the cakes are eaten, blow out the moon candle. Then pour the melted wax from it into the water. It will cool quickly. Use it to divine from, to see what the next month will bring. For young children, this is a game of "What does it look like?"

As the children go to bed, anoint them with the water, saying:

> *May the Moon send you good dreams.*

The moon water can also be used for sprinklings, offerings, or watering plants.

These are some alternative prayers that can be used either after the candle lighting or while the cakes are passed out:

> *Mother Moon*
> *Watch over us*
> *Mother Moon*
> *Keep us safe*
> *Mother Moon*
> *Wrap us in your arms*
> *Mother Moon*
> *Shine brightly on our way.*

Mother of All, worthy of great honor,
watch over us as the month goes by
and bring us to the next Full Moon
safe and healthy and happy.

Traditions to raid: Chinese Moon Festival (Chung Chiu).

The New Moon

The new moon can mean different things to different people. To some it is the dark time, the three days of moonless nights when the moon changes from waxing to waning. Or it can mean the first sliver of the waxing moon that shows itself just after sunset and disappears soon after.

When most Neo-Pagans say it they mean the dark time. This is a time of great mystery, when deep changes take place in the souls of women and men who are in tune with it. These are personal mysteries, private changes, and are especially appropriate for adolescents, who are undergoing their own mysterious changes. For younger children, don't play too heavily on them. Their time will come.

The ritual includes a strong symbol of the moon hidden away and an emphasis on dreams. These will plant the seed, which is what we want most for our children when they are young.

The Dark Moon

Again use your best plates and serve lunar foods. This time use darker food and drink, such as red wine or iced tea. For cakes use something dark, hermits or oatmeal or chocolate cookies, or gingerbread, for instance, or something else made with molasses or brown sugar. Put the moon candle in the center of the table. Don't light any candles. In front of one of the children's plates put a square or circle of black or dark blue cloth. (If you have more than one child, take turns.) A dark cloth napkin will do. Establish sacred time, but without lighting any candles.

Ritual 1

At a sign from one of the adults, one of the children says:

> *Why is tonight special?*

An adult answers:

> *Tonight is the Dark Moon.*

The child (or another one) says:

> *Why is this a special time?*

An adult answers:

> *The Dark Moon is the Alone Time,*
> *time to be by yourself in quiet,*
> *to dream of the changes you are going through*
> *and to honor the changes you have made*
> *since the last time the Moon was dark.*

As with the Full Moon, the questions can be asked by the adults and the answers given by the children.

The child who has the cloth in front of her picks it up, holds it over the moon candle, and drops it. She arranges it so that it completely covers the candle. Then the mother holds her hands over the candle and says:

> *The sky is dark*
> *with no Moon to be seen.*
> *She is hidden in secret*
> *to make Herself new.*
> *The Moon is dark tonight*
> *as She passes from light to light.*

Ritual 2

With everything arranged as before, one of the adults says:

> *Shh.*
> *It is dark tonight*
> *with no moon to light our way.*
> *Shh.*

The child covers the candle. One of the parents says:

> *The sky will be dark tonight,*
> *with no moon to light our way.*
> *She is hidden in the dark*
> *to make herself new*
> *and then return*
> *young and bright and dancing in the sky.*

After the ritual, eat your meal. After that, no matter which ritual is used, one adult says:

> *Dark time*
> *Quiet time*
> *Sleep time*
> *Dream time*
> *Time of change.*
> *Sleep well tonight*
> *with wonderful dreams.*

Then put the candle back in the shrine, still wrapped in the cloth. One of the children can do this. Alternatively, it can be kept on the table as a reminder of the dark time. Or it can be kept in the shrine and moved to the table for meals.

The Reappearance of the Moon

The reappearance of the moon was celebrated by Paleo-Pagans more than the dark time. Sometimes contests would be held among villagers, the winner being the one who saw the moon first. *Carmina Gadelica* (see References) gives a number of beautiful Gaelic prayers for this day. It is a day well suited for family celebration, especially if you have a clear view of where the moon will appear. If you can't find the moon on its first night because of intervening objects or bad weather, try on subsequent nights until you can see it.

Go outside right before sunset. In a city you can use a balcony or a roof, or even an open window. (It is considered bad luck to seek the moon first through glass.) Bring with you the wrapped moon candle. If you have the moon ribbon braid suggested above bring it and attach it to a stick. Otherwise use another stick, decorated with mirrors, silver jewelry, and white, silver, and blue ribbons. Face west and watch for the sun to set and the moon to appear. (Don't look straight at the sun!) As the light fades, the moon will become visible above where the sun set. The first one who sees it gets to take the stick and point to the moon. She then takes the moon candle, unwraps it, holds it up to the moon, and says:

> *She's back!*
> *Welcome back, Moon.*
> *Thank you for returning to us.*

Putting both stick and candle down, she kisses her hand to the moon. Then everyone else does. The candle and stick are brought inside and put on the table. If she is an adult (anyone who has come of age) she lights it. If not, the mother lights it. While it is being lit, the one who saw the moon says:

> *The Moon is back*
> *and a New Moon begins.*
> *New things will happen.*

The mother then says:

> *Think about it:*
> *What new things do you want to happen*
> *   in the New Moon?*
> *What new things will you make happen*
> *   in the New Moon?*

The members of the family can then either say what they plan for the new moon or not as they wish. (Remember the embarrassment factor.) This is a good time for vows. For instance, "I will meditate daily for this month." If there are other Pagan families near you, gather together and have a contest for seeing the moon first. The winning family keeps the moon braid for the month. For a less complicated new moon observance, after everyone is at the table for dinner that night, one of the adults asks:

Has anyone seen the Moon tonight?

If no one has, then everyone can go out to look. If more than one person has, you can compare times to see who saw it first. (This can become quite a competition.) Whoever sees it first gets to put the moon candle on the table and uncover it. If the child is old enough he then lights it; if not, the mother does. The same person also gets to blow the candle out at the end of the meal.

For either ritual, have a small bowl of oil, scented or olive, on the table. Hold it over the lit candle for a few seconds and then anoint each others' foreheads with it, saying:

May She be with you this month
and smile on you every day.

❦ 9 ❧

Coming of Age

Something our culture does not do well is to help our children make the transition to adulthood. We do our best to raise them, but they are never quite sure if they have earned adulthood. The crisis is especially acute among males, and is the source of much machismo with all the suffering that brings, both for the males and for those they come in contact with. If coming of age rituals are not provided by adults, they will be created by adolescents. The results are such disasters as street gangs and train surfers.

An effective coming of age starts young. Children are shown how adults act, are told the responsibilities and privileges that come with adulthood, and are taught about the changes they will undergo during puberty. An eight year old who has discussed both the physical and spiritual side of menstruation with both of her parents is less likely to be embarrassed by a coming of age than one who has not discussed it at all or who has discussed it only with her mother. A boy who has learned that responsibility comes with manhood is likely to accept that manhood when its responsibilities are given to him and then carried out.

Coming of age is not just a ritual. It is a process that takes place over a number of years and for some of us never ends or ends too late. A rite of passage is a good beginning, though, and for a well-prepared youth it may be enough.

One function such a ritual accomplishes is to show the importance of coming of age. It is an acknowledgement that the community considers growing up important, so important that it will help acknowledge and celebrate the youth's accomplishment.

The ritual may sometimes be merely a formalization of growing up already done. It may also be the beginning of a process about to start. And it may give direction to something that has started already. What it is not is a mere ceremony, like a graduation ceremony. It is a ritual, and it has effects on all levels. It is a magical act, and it has magical effects.

Pagan cultures are very good at marking comings of age. Studies of these rituals fill many books and journals with accounts of ordeals and celebrations. There are patterns in them that we need to use ourselves.

A coming of age ritual begins with a separation. In both boys and girls this will be a separation from childhood, in boys it will mean separation from the world of the female as well. (Even in two-career families the home is equated with mother.) This is especially difficult for Pagans, since we revere the female as sacred. How is the boy to separate without learning distrust? How is he to separate without becoming alienated from the Goddess?

Initiatory separation is frequently involuntary, sometimes amounting to a kidnaping. The child is brought to a sacred space, where he is tested and taught the ways of adulthood. At the end of this is an acceptance as a man or woman by the same sex group, followed by a reincorporation into the society as a whole, along with a recognition by the opposite sex.

This pattern has to be modified somewhat to apply today. It is simply not possible to fit everything an adult has to know into one period of seclusion. That period would have to be several years long, something that would hardly serve the purpose of preparing the child to function in society. Instead we have adolescence. Is it any wonder adolescents are confused and frequently in psychological pain? They are in the midst of the ordeals of their rites of passage, and there are no elders to show them the way.

If it is not possible to use the coming of age ritual to teach our children all they need to know, we can at least mark the beginning and end of the transitionary period. We can push them into their adolescence, guide them through it, and welcome and acknowledge them at the end. This requires two rituals, separated by a period of years during which the child can mature and be instructed. The first takes place at the entry into adolescence, for the girl at menarche, and for the boy whenever it seems appropriate. Thirteen is a good age for boys, although some may be ready earlier or later. If a physical sign is desired, the time can be when the boy's voice starts to change.

More than anything else in this book, these rituals are written in an ideal form. They require much: land, a community, and a child who is ready for them. If it is possible to perform them as written, then do so. If it is not (and be honest; sometimes "not possible" just means "incredibly inconvenient"), then substitute. The important factors are a separation from childhood, a test, teaching, and acceptance as an adult by other adults.

The needs of boys and girls, and the nature of their sacred power, are sufficiently different that their coming of age rituals must also be different. These are rituals of coming into sexual power, and each sex has its unique form of this power. Each sex also needs its own way of coming into power.

Both rituals end in a party. Parties are one way our culture has of saying that something is worth celebrating. Presents are given. These can include a bag of money to buy an athame with (if the family is Wiccan), a drum (if the family is shamanic), and a key to the house. Even if the child has a key already, a new one is presented ritually. This is a sign of being able to come and go. New women are given garnet, pearl, or moonstone jewelry, in honor of their bleeding and connection with the moon. A new man may be given a gold pendant, in honor of his new ability to act in the God's place. After the giving of gifts there is dancing, both sacred and secular.

As well as receiving presents, the new adult must give some. He gives away some of his childhood books and toys to younger children as both a rite of separation from childhood and the assumption of adult responsibilities to care for children.

Don't limit yourself to religious rites. Is there something you've told your child she could only do when she was old enough? A camping trip, ear piercing, wearing high heels or pearls, going somewhere alone, staying up past a certain time, being allowed to wear makeup or a two-piece bathing suit, having a perm—these all can be rites of passage and something should be made of them. They are all things that can say to your child, "You are old enough. You have crossed a threshold."

Traditions to raid: Roman Catholic confirmation, Baptist baptism, Jewish bar and bat mitzvahs.

Before going to the location where the ritual will take place, the adolescent cuts his or her hair. This could be as drastic a cut as he or she thinks right. The hair is laid before the family shrine overnight, with these words:

> *Guardians of my childhood,*
> *I give you this gift,*
> *growth of my childhood.*
> *I am leaving my childhood behind*
> *but still wish your protection.*

In the morning the hair is taken outside and burned.

After the ritual the new adult again visits the household shrine, and this time gives an offering of incense.

Girl's Puberty Ritual

As in many traditions, the girl initiate is shut off from light for most of the ritual. In some cultures this is an attempt to prevent impregnation by the sun during this vulnerable time. Other meanings are more relevant here, though. The girl in the dark is separated from male space: she does not see the sun, the preeminent God symbol. She is in the dark womb, waiting to be reborn. She is in the chrysalis, undergoing metamorphosis. She is by herself, without even the light to show her other things. She is out of time, separate from the passage of the sun through the sky, and thus she is in the Original Time, the Beginning Time, the Dream Time, where the world is begun. She is present at That Time, and it will give birth to her as a woman.

A woman may choose to return to the hut of seclusion at times crucial to her spirituality. Such huts are famous for being used during menstruation. They were not meant as a punishment, or as an expression of spiritual pollution coming from a menstruating woman. Like the original Polynesian concept of tabu, the idea is protection of the rest of us. There is great magic here that must be brought under control. The new woman will have power, but the power is for the good of society. The seclusion hut keeps society safe from the sudden unleashing of that power.

There is still more to this, though. The hut (and it could be as large as desired) is female space. In small groups it is not uncommon for all the women to menstruate at the same time. The hut then becomes a place for women to gather and celebrate the mysteries of womanhood. Its presence in the puberty rite is the first introduction of the girl to this. Even if she has been part of a Pagan community, she has not been allowed into women's mysteries before. Now she will be, and will know that she is grown up by that very fact.

One more way of looking at the hut is as an incubator of the new woman she is becoming. Here there are no distractions to give her an excuse not to do the hard work she is about to do. She has no choice. Which of us does have a choice about whether to grow up? But how many of us still try not to?

A new woman has proof of her new status. She has begun to menstruate, she has become part of the turning. What she needs to do is go into herself and ask what that means. So she goes into the hut and goes into herself. The mother may come in and talk and paint designs. Others who have gone this way may give advice. But in the end it is solely up to the new woman. All by herself she sits in the hut and asks herself the questions. Who am I? What am I becoming? How will I do that? How will I know?

The hut itself prevents the new woman from looking outside herself for her power. Later, when she is secure in her self, she may wish to go out on quest to see what mountain and tree have to tell her. For now, though, she has the harder task of finding her purpose in her own self. It would be too easy to grasp something outside of her; to help her resist the temptation, the number of outside stimuli is reduced. For the night, it is just her in the hut. If she is to find meaning, that is where she will find it.

This ritual closely parallels one performed by some tribes along the northern coast of Australia. That it was written before encountering the Australian rite shows clearly the universality of initiatory themes.

It would work best if done at a women's gathering, or at a Pagan gathering with women's space. It is written for a place that has a lake or pond where outside nudity is possible. It can be adapted to other circumstances (I will give suggestions for this at the end), but finding a way to do it as written would really be best.

Choose a woman to serve as the girl's guardian. She might be the same woman chosen as her guardian at her dedication or another woman. Choose someone trusted by both you and your daughter. It will be her job to guide the child through adolescence, answering all the questions the child is too embarrassed to ask her mother.

Ritual

The seclusion hut is preferably built like a sweat lodge (without the hot stones) or a wigwam, but a dark enough tent will do. (Make sure it is not airtight.)

At sunset the girl goes to it, accompanied by the women who will take part in the later part of the ritual. She is naked (skyclad). (If you cannot achieve sufficient privacy, she can disrobe immediately in front of the entrance to the hut.) As the women walk with her, they say:

> *The butterfly enters the chrysalis,*
> *The seed enters the ground,*
> *The child enters the womb,*
> *To be transformed*
> *To be transformed.*

She is left there for the night. Before she is left her mother says:

> *You are becoming a woman*
> *and now you must find your way.*
> *Go deep, daughter.*
> *The only way out is through.*

The girl must open the door and enter without any help or coercion. Once inside, she sits facing away from the door. She sits there for the night by herself—meditating, thinking, wondering, fasting, and just plain worrying. The worrying is OK; it builds tension which will intensify the ritual. She does her best to stay awake.

Finally, at dawn, her mother joins her, carrying a candle and body paint and bringing water to drink. When she enters she allows as little light as possible to enter. She tells her daughter stories of the daughter's childhood and the mother's teen years. As she talks she paints designs on her daughter's body with the paint, appropriate to the story being told. If she has had a secret name given her at her saining, it is now revealed to her, along with its meaning and the reason it was given. It is written on her body with the paint. Throughout the day, periods of teaching and talking alternate with periods of seclusion. This continues until dark.

After dark the mother blindfolds the girl and leaves. The girl's guardian comes in and leads her to the beach and out to water about waist deep. Other significant women in the girl's life (adult friends, relatives, friends who have already gone through the ritual) have gathered skyclad and lined up one behind the other in the water, facing the shore, their legs spread apart. Her mother or her guardians asks:

Who were you?

She answers with names she was known by in childhood. Her mother or her guardian asks:

Who are you?

She answers with the name by which she wishes to be known as a woman. It might be the name she has been known by before or one that has come to her in her meditating. After she answers, she is pulled into the water by her guardian and then must crawl/swim through their legs (helped by them and her guardian). As she goes through each woman's legs, that woman says:

(Her new name) *is born.*
A woman is born.

Her mother is last and she helps her to her feet. The mother towels her off, wiping off any marks that may still be on her. Her blindfold is removed and she is wrapped up in a blanket and carried to the door of the building where the party will be.

At the door, she is set down on her feet. A moon crown is placed on her head, a cup in her right hand, and an ear of corn in her left. A necklace is placed around her neck, and the women bow to her, saying:

> *You are the Mother of All.*
> *From you are born the peoples of the Earth.*

Each woman draws a symbol of the Goddess on her with body paint, explaining it as she does so. They then have her turn to face the door and spread her legs. They crawl thorough her legs into the building. She follows them.

What happens next is up to the women, but it should include elemental blessings. This is also the time to talk about womanhood and sexuality from a sacred perspective.

When this is done and the women are dressed again (the new woman in something special) but things are still going on, a signal is given to the outside (without the new woman's knowledge) and men come, chanting, drumming, and dancing. These are men who are significant in the new woman's life (her father, other male relatives, friends of the family). They are challenged at the door but finally admitted. The new woman has to give permission before they can enter.

When both parents are present, they give a blessing to the new woman. This may be a short prayer or a ritual purification. It should express hope for a happy and productive life.

The ritual can be performed indoors if necessary. It should be in a house or apartment other than the girl's, to emphasize that she is leaving her childhood behind. The hut can be replaced by a room that has been completely emptied and had blackout curtains put on the windows. A freestanding tent is even better, again in a dark room. The bathtub can be used to immerse the girl, with the crowning as Goddess either in that room or in another. If nudity is not possible or desirable, the girl can wear white or unbleached natural fiber cloth. She should still be nude while in the hut, however, disrobing upon entering it and being dressed when leaving. The other women can wear the clothing they would wear to any celebration for the party and bathing suits for the immersion.

Boy's Puberty Ritual

The classic boy's coming of age ritual consists of a forceable separation from boyhood and his mother by divine beings, usually the ancestors, who test him, teach him, and accept him. The ancestors can be either of two types, the biological or the mythological. The meaning in either case is that these are the ones who have done these things before and have made them sacred. These are men, and they are the ones who can make the boy a man. They are the fathers, whose approval is necessary if the boy is to grow up.

A boy's coming of age of necessity involves more of an ordeal than a girl's. The boy does not have the major body signals to convince him that he has indeed become a man. He must feel tested and he must feel that he has passed that test. Anything else will leave him in doubt of his manhood. There must be no doubt; that is the whole point of having this ritual in the first place.

The adolescent boy must be accepted by the world of the fathers. If separation from the mother is not done he will do it himself, with adolescent rebellion and all its dangers. (Perhaps the dangers are its appeal. He seeks an ordeal.) If he is not ritually accepted by the fathers, he will spend his life trying to prove his adulthood, with all the dangers for society (and himself) that this entails.

This is why there must be fathers to be accepted by in the ritual. It is most important for the boy's own father to be there. If that is absolutely impossible, the father's part must be taken by an adult male whom the boy respects and to whom he is close. If there is no one who fills this role, the ritual will not work. A boy needs a male role model to grow up. If he has none, growing up will last into adult life and may never be done at all.

In Celtic myth there is a tradition of youths being given their adult names and their weapons by their mothers. This reflects nicely the Pagan belief that power has its source in the Goddess.

But among the Lakota, young men took their names from something important they had done or that came to them in their vision quests. The point here is that manhood is something which must be seized; it is not something given.

The Lakota way reflects well the experience of becoming a man in America. Boys feel they must earn the right to manhood and would not accept it if offered freely. Whether this is good or bad I will not debate here. But that this is the way it is can be demonstrated in the lives of almost all men. If you wish to change this, a puberty rite is too late. (I doubt whether it can be changed at all; the pressures of society are very strong.) A puberty rite must work, and it must work with what it has. Choose your symbols carefully to create the effect you want.

Ritual

It is best to perform this rite at a Pagan gathering. This provides an appropriate place, a group of interested adults, and some time before the ritual in a sacred environment. If this is not possible, perform it during some sort of vacation, a camping trip perhaps. This will serve to mark the time and place as special, outside the ordinary routine.

As soon as possible after arriving at the gathering, hold a sweat lodge. This is intended to purify the boy and to impress on him the seriousness of the coming ritual. If it is not possible to build a sweat lodge, or if no one present is sufficiently experienced to run one, perform some other purification ritual, preferably involving water. A sauna makes a good substitute for a sweat lodge, provided it is held in a ritual manner. Part of the purification rite is a removal of his name:

> *Your name has been eaten.*
> *You are in-between:*
> *Nameless, unborn, unfinished.*

From this point until the naming in the ritual he is addressed by everyone as "boy."

After the purification rite or sweat lodge, give the boy something to mark that he is a candidate for initiation. This could be a special article of clothing, or a piece of jewelry, or especially a mark such as a white streak across his face. Restrict his diet. If he is an omnivore, he might be forbidden to eat meat. If he is a vegetarian, he might be required to eat meat. Other possibilities include androgynous clothing, undyed clothing, eating only with his fingers, restrictions on speaking, and eating mainly dairy products. Each of these has its own meaning. In androgynous clothing he is marked as neither male nor female, the original state in the womb before differentiation. Undyed clothing is a sign of the untransformed person. Eating with fingers is the mark of the unacculturated. Babies and the unborn do not speak. Milk is the food of infants. In these ways he is marked as someone who is about to be reborn and separated from those who aren't.

At some point during the gathering, without warning or the boy's knowledge of the exact time, he is kidnapped by the initiating men. This is done at sunset. If it can be contrived for the boy to be watching the sunset with his mother and younger siblings, so much the better. At the least he should be with his mother.

A cloth bag (not plastic) or blanket is thrown over his head from behind and he is brought, perhaps carried, perhaps dragged, to the initiatory cabin. This can be any structure, a cabin, tent, or house, as long as it is big enough. It must be set off in some way, in the wilds apart from other buildings.

When the initiate is inside, the bag or blanket is removed. Around him are the men who have brought him there. They are all masked. They represent the ancestors. In front of him is a man, preferably his father. He must be a man whom the boy regards as a role model. He wears a God mask. This could be a Cernunnos mask, complete with antlers, or a Kachina mask, or a Green Man mask, or any kind that fits with the tradition of the family. If the ancestors are represented in the family shrine by full size masks, the male ancestor mask is a good choice. What is important is that it completely disguise its wearer and that it be instantly recognizable by the boy as the mask of a male sacred being. This man says:

> *You have been brought here*
> *into the dark*
> *to where the ancestors wait,*
> *all the men who have gone this way before you;*
> *to where the God waits,*
> *He who began this way and who is its guardian.*
> *You have been brought to your testing place.*
> *Do you wish the test?*

He replies in the affirmative. The man continues:

> *You have been brought here*
> *into the dark*
> *where demons lurk*
> *where the unknown lives*
> *where dangers hide in the shadows.*
> *You have been brought to your testing place.*
> *Do you wish the test?*

He again replies. The man continues:

> *You have been brought here*
> *into the dark*
> *the dark of the womb*
> *which gives birth*
> *the dark of the earth*
> *which receives you at death*
> *the dark of grave and cave*
> *which hold mysteries dark and deep.*
> *You have been brought to your testing place.*
> *Do you wish the test?*

He again replies. The man continues:

> *You have been brought here against your will.*
> *No one asked you to come to this point in your life.*
> *But you have decided to undergo the testing.*
> *There was no choice but to be presented with the test*
> *To undergo it was your own choice.*
> *Hear me, ancestors.*
> *Hear me, men.*
> *I give him over to you to be tested.*

The ancestors strip the boy and make him white with ashes or powdered chalk. They say:

> *The boy has died.*
> *He has gone into the dark.*
> *There is no way out but through.*

They may say this once or repeat it over and over as they paint him. When they are done he is led into the wild. There he spends the night alone. Before they leave the ancestors wrap him in a blanket. Although this serves the practical purpose of making the ordeal less severe, it also has the symbolic value of standing for the amniotic sac, or caul. Among some people, to be born still in this sac is a sign of special power.

He spends the night alone in vision quest. He must stay awake all night and see what comes to him. If against all his efforts he falls asleep he must remember his dreams.

In the morning, during false dawn, he is brought to a place from which the rising sun can be seen. The men once again have their ancestor masks on. The man in the God mask is not there. The boy is brought blindfolded and in silence. It is best if the last stretch is up a hill. (It is in the high places that the god of sky and sun is encountered.) At the end of the walk he is faced east and the blindfold is removed so that he sees the rising sun. When the sun has risen all the way, what is left of the white is wiped off. The blanket is put back on for a second and then removed. In this way his final birth is enacted. He is then turned to face west (thereby standing in the direction of birth, facing towards his death, having been reborn like the sun). The God figure from before is there now. He says:

> *You have returned from the night.*
> *What vision have you brought us?*

The boy then tells what happened on his quest. From the vision(s) the man in the mask derives a name. He says:

> *The man has had a vision*
> *The man has found a name*
> *You are* (name)
> *You are a man.*

The boy then goes from man to man. Each removes his mask and hugs the initiate, saying:

> *Welcome,* (old name).
> *Welcome,* (new name).
> *Welcome to manhood.*

After he has been welcomed by all the other men he is brought by them to the man in the God mask. The man in the mask calls him by his new name. When the initiate answers, the man says:

> *You have been called.*
> *You have answered.*
> *You have done what needed to be done.*
> *You have gone through.*
> *You have endured within.*
> *You have come out.*
> *And here you stand on the other side.*
> *A man.*
> *Welcome,* (new name).
> *Welcome.*

He takes off the mask and gives it to the initiate, who puts it on. The new man faces each of the other men, who salute him in turn. He finally faces the sun for a second and then takes the mask off and hands it back to his father.

After the new man has been dressed in new clothes, there is a procession, with much noise—drums, bells, bullroarers—to where the women and children wait. The new man is greeted by the women and a party is held with presents and dancing. At the party the new man is blessed by his parents in the same way a new woman would be.

After the party, the men gather again in the cabin or tent where the ritual started. The new man is of course there. They drum and dance and talk, teaching the new man what it is to be a man. Subjects can include sex, jobs, the proper treatment of women, fatherhood, homosexuality, the nature of masculinity, and even those topics stereotypically associated with men—sports, finance, etc. The meeting goes on for as long as is necessary, and both begins and ends in drumming.

In the days after the ritual the new man makes a mask of his own. He must take part in the next coming of age, this time as one of the initiators. In this way he begins to take on the sacred responsibilities of being a man, and acknowledges that the way a student repays his debt to his teachers is by passing the teaching on.

Transition

After the first ritual the new adult is considered an adult for all religious purposes. He may take the adult parts in family celebrations. He may serve as a guardian in a dedication. If the family has had family membership in any religious organizations he is now responsible for his own membership.

The new adult has had her power awakened and acknowledged. She has not come into her full power, however, nor does she know how to use it fully. She still has much to learn about the world. There is need for a period of transition before the final ritual.

This is a time of further training. Although the child is now spiritually an adult she still must be trained in the skills required to fully attain the status of adulthood. This includes training in practical things: finances, cooking, self-defense, home repair, driving, auto repair, work, education, etc. She may also wish to deepen her vision by going on a vision quest, a time by herself to explore who it is she is becoming.

The new woman should be trained in the mother's part in the family rituals. She might wear her mother's moon crown or have one given to her or made by her. Alternatively, she might make her own when she establishes her own household. The new man would of course be trained in the father's part in the family rituals.

Don't just perform the coming of age ritual and go back to your relationship as it was. If the ritual worked, that won't be possible anyway. Your new adult will need a new relationship. She is not all grown up but a new phase of training and recognition has begun.

Bring the child more into family decisions. Teach her about home finances and ask her advice. If you practice shamanism, this is the time to start teaching your child how to journey. A Wiccan family might invite the new adult into circle and start preparing her for initiation.

The adult that the child is becoming is part of a society. During this period, therefore, he must involve himself in community work. This may be anything from volunteering at a shelter for the homeless to lobbying for recycling. It should be something that requires him to work with other people.

He must also get a paying job as soon as he is old enough. He can spend part of his money, but some goes to his family as his contribution and some is saved for education. He is learning to be responsible for himself.

Rite of Completion

The second rite is an acknowledgement that the necessary learning has been accomplished and that the initiate has come into her full power. There will still be learning and growing to do, of course, right up until death, but a major point has been passed. This second rite should be performed after high school graduation, right before the child leaves home for college or her own place to live.

The ritual begins with a three-day vision quest, the goal of which is to determine her goals for life, both mundane and spiritual. (These goals will change as she grows, of course.) The place and time are picked by her, and she is responsible for organizing it. During her quest she spends the time alone, preferably in a wild place. She doesn't go without support, of course. She takes the standard camping equipment, including a whistle or siren with which to signal a helper who stays separately but within hearing. This person can be her guardian or another person on vision quest, but it must not be one of her parents. She is learning to get by on her own, and that is tough to do when Mommy or Daddy are within earshot. A way of communicating, perhaps by leaving a message at a landmark, is arranged with the helper. The quester will need to leave a message each day so that the helper will know she is safe. Simply being alone and fasting is enough of a challenge; we are trying to create adults, not martyrs.

The last day of the quest is spent fasting from food. In her poverty she cries for help, asking for vision. She waits for knowledge to come to her from the emptiness as to the direction she should take after the ritual.

Before she leaves for her quest, she receives a blessing from her parents. She also gives an offering to the guardians of the household. As part of this, she explains what she is about to do, and asks for their blessings in the future, even though she must go.

On returning from her quest, she is greeted by her parents. They say to her:

You who have come from the wild,
shining with the power of the Gods.
We see your power, fully awakened in you.
Come to us, from your place of power,
and give us your blessing.

She blesses them, and then is invited by them to a party in her honor. At the party, she gives them presents bought before the quest with her own money or made by her during the quest. She says to them:

You have given me much
and I wish to give you something.

They reply:

You have already given us much
but we accept this with gratitude.

When the time has come for the child to leave (and it is best if she not stay the night), the parents say to her:

What we have taught you is not yours to keep.
We ourselves did not have it to own
but only to guard until time to pass it on.
Now these teachings are yours
and the responsibility is yours as well
to keep the teaching and to pass it on.
Do it well.

She replies:

I will.

They say to her:

I am your father forever
I am your mother forever
No matter where you go
and who you become
we will always be your parents.

She replies:

Though now I am an adult,
I am still your child.
No matter where I go
and who I become
I will always be your child.
I will not forget what I have learned here.

❧ 10 ❧

Betrothal, Wedding, Parting

W hen children grow up, they leave home. Some leave to set up households as individuals. Some move in with friends. And some get married. Yes, they do, as hard as it may be to believe when your children are small.

A parent has a delicate position in such matters. Some try to take over their child's wedding completely. The unfortunate ones succeed. But just as each member of a married couple is a blend of family traditions and unique qualities, about to be joined with another such blend, so too should be their wedding. It is *their* wedding, mothers and fathers, and although you will get your say, they get the last word. You trust them enough to *be* married; surely you can trust them with the *getting* married part.

My advice up to this point of the book has been directed at telling adults what can be done with children. Adults, this is my advice: turn the wedding over to the children. I am turning this chapter over to them.

Of course, marriage is a family affair, make no doubt about that. Family members of all generations come together not only to watch but to participate. Their very presence is an affirmation of the couple and of marriage in general. The gathering of generations almost guarantees the presence of non-Pagans at the wedding. It is a good time for introducing non-Pagan relatives to your ways. A beautiful wedding can draw in the most stubborn of objectors.

Remember this as you plan the ritual, and remember that little things may make all the difference in the world. Talk to people who will be guests and whose opinion you value. Listen for key phrases such as "It just isn't a wedding without …" or "I love it at weddings when …" It may turn out that all it takes to placate Great-aunt Olive is the right kind of cake. A good marriage is a compromise. A wedding is a good place to start.

I am not saying that you should compromise your religious values, of course. You have every right to be married in a Pagan way. But please keep in mind that a wedding belongs in part to the community and that they should have their say as well. If you want these people there, surely you want their approval.

Betrothal

It is customary in many cultures for a wedding to have two parts, the betrothal and the wedding itself, with a period between them that may last for days or for years. The traditional length for a Pagan betrothal is a year and a day, although the time may vary according to a couple's needs. In our culture the place of betrothal is taken by engagement, a serious step with certain privileges and responsibilities that can be broken but only with some difficulty.

"Handfasting" was originally a form of betrothal, a trial marriage, for a year and a day, at the end of which it was dissolved or made permanent. The name of this Gaelic tradition has become the Neo-Pagan term for a wedding, and a very pretty word it is too. However, it should still be remembered that the original tradition was one of betrothal, and while "handfasting" may now mean "wedding" there should still be a betrothal.

The customs used by popular culture to mark the betrothed status, such as engagement rings, are in keeping with Pagan tradition, although it would be better for such gifts to be mutual. The exchange of such tokens is a part of betrothal everywhere. In many places, the traditional token is a broken coin, of which each party keeps half. Other popular tokens include belts and bracelets. The symbolism of binding, enclosing, and the infinity of the circle is common to many of these.

The decision to marry is, of course, a private one, made at a private moment. After the decision is made, though, the couple should gather both families together to announce it. The tokens may be exchanged at this time, with a kiss. Toasts are made to the couple. Before the toasts, the parents tie the couple's hands together with a natural fiber cord, saying:

> *Now you are bound,*
> *one to the other,*
> *with a tie not easy to break.*
> *Take this time of binding*
> *before the final vows are made*
> *to learn what you need to know*
> *to grow in wisdom and love*
> *that your marriage might be strong*
> *that your love might last.*

The cord is left on for the toasts and then removed by the parents and given to the couple to be kept safe.

Offerings are made to the family guardians. The images can be brought to the announcement ritual or the couple can present themselves next time they visit their parents' homes. They take this time to introduce the new family members to the guardians. If it is impossible to gather the families, the announcement should still be made in front of witnesses.

Wedding

A wedding is not just an agreement between two people. It is effective on three planes, the individual, the social, and the cosmic.

That marriage affects the individual plane is obvious. That it affects the social plane will be made painfully clear by the family of the bride and the groom. Have patience with them; a wedding is an important step in the continuation of the community. But it is on the cosmic plane that Pagan weddings come into their own.

A bride and a groom stand at the moment of creation. Through them the world is renewed. They are Queen and King, Priestess and Priest, Goddess and God. In ancient Greece, weddings imitated the wedding of Zeus and Hera. The Hindu wedding ceremony has the groom say to his bride, "I am heaven, thou art earth." And in the ritual which will be given here, the bride and groom are consecrated as divinities and given homage.

Since a wedding is a new beginning, elements of wedding rituals frequently are shared with New Years' rituals and vice versa. In ancient Sumer, for instance, the ritual for New Year's climaxed in a reenactment of the creation story which included a marriage between the king and the Goddess, between earth and heaven. This is the sort of thing which a bride and groom are getting themselves into.

The ceremony requires a Priest and a Priestess. In many areas of the country it is possible to find Pagan Priests and Priestesses legally qualified to perform wedding ceremonies. If this is not true where you live, or if you wish to have someone not legally qualified officiate, a civil wedding can be performed either before or after the religious one, with only the minimum number of people attending. That will prevent the civil wedding from being seen as the "real" wedding.

The bride and groom should approach the wedding with a combination of joy and fear. It is only right that this should be so; a wedding is a cusp, an initiation, a moment when a couple's lives will be changed forever. This proper state should not be too hard to achieve; it is, after all, the natural state of brides and grooms.

The bride and groom should spend the night before the wedding separately. They are going to come together from their aloneness. They should spend at least part of it in meditation, alone or with a few friends, to prepare themselves spiritually. When they get up on the day of the wedding, the bride and groom should perform whatever purification ritual their tradition uses.

If they do not have one that they usually use, they can start with a bath, with cleansing herbs if they like (yarrow and hawthorn are traditional wedding herbs). Then they can meditate for a while, which will also help them calm themselves. They should call upon the God and Goddess to bless the wedding and the marriage. If they still live at home or are leaving for the wedding from home, they must pray to the family guardians, asking peace between the guardians and them as they move out and found their own family. The guardians should be given a last offering of incense and hair before leaving.

Since from that morning they start a new life, they should fast, consuming only milk, the food of babies. This Roman custom also introduces one of the themes of this ritual. Dionysus is usually thought of as the god of wine, and indeed he is. But he is also the god of faithful marriage. After Theseus had abandoned Ariadne, Dionysus found her. They were married and he was faithful to her, not a common state of things among the Greco-Roman deities. He is also god of liquids, especially those that flow through and from living things. He is therefore called upon in this wedding ritual through the three liquids that will be drunk.

Wedding dates are often a matter of convenience. If possible, though, the date should be significant. Lammas (August 1st) is the traditional date in Scotland. In Ireland it was the date of the year and a day trial marriage at Tailteann. A fair was held there on Lammas where marriages were arranged which could be dissolved at the next fair. May Day and Midsummers are also good; in some Neo-Pagan traditions one or the other of these days is celebrated as the wedding day of the Goddess and the God. (The Romans considered May to be an unlucky month for weddings, giving rise to the June wedding tradition, but in Paganism as it is practiced today May Day is perfectly suitable.) If none of these is practical, make an effort to schedule the wedding for the waxing of the moon, especially the day the new moon is first visible—as the moon grows, so might the marriage.

Dress for weddings is a personal choice. Some Pagans wear ritual garb, while others will choose the traditional American clothes. The white dress is not inappropriate for a Pagan wedding. Contrary to popular opinion, the wearing of white has nothing to do with virginity, but is only limited to first weddings. White is a traditional color for initiations and new beginnings. Unless all your friends and relatives are Pagans or nudists it is unlikely that nudity will be an option.

There is no Pagan reason to refrain from most of the customs that surround weddings in our culture. It is true, of course, that some of these traditions may have meanings a Pagan will find offensive. If something offends you, don't do it. But if you really want to do something but wonder what the other Pagans would think, you are missing the point of tradition. Many traditions are done because they're what's done in a particular situation. "This is what my parents did" is a perfectly Pagan sentiment. Does anybody *really* think of the meaning of being carried over the threshold while it's being done? If you find meaning in something (and simply being fun is meaning enough), then do it. Reinterpret it if necessary, but do it.

Many wedding traditions of the various ethnic groups in our country are also appropriate at a Pagan wedding (and may go far towards making peace with a family upset at a Pagan ceremony). Throwing grain, a wedding cake, traditional dances—there is nothing inherently un-Pagan about these. Some of them are in fact of Pagan origin.

Weather permitting, Pagan weddings should be outside, touching the ground and under the gaze of the sky. If this is not possible, the couple should go outside at some point after the ceremony to call on earth and sky as witnesses.

Ritual

Few Pagans have the luxury of a temple or other sacred space large enough to hold a wedding of any size. It will therefore usually be necessary to consecrate the area where the ceremony will take place. A circle will need to be cast.

This circle is not one to keep power in or spirits out. If the bulk of the guests are outside the circle, it is especially important that the circle not keep things out. It is instead an area of space that has been blessed and declared sacred. The spirits of the four directions are called and reverenced, but no wall is established between the sacred and profane worlds.

In the place where the ritual will be, form a circle from flowers to mark the sacred area. Guests can stand outside or inside the flower circle, depending on how many guests and flowers you have. Chairs should be provided for those who need them. If the day is hot, there should definitely be seats, and an awning for shade may be necessary as well. Chairs will also be necessary if guests are dressed in the usual American wedding clothes, which aren't well-suited for either standing or sitting on the ground. The bulk of the guests should be sitting or standing in the south to allow room in the north for the ritual to take place.

The altar is put in the center of the circle. It can be any table of a convenient height that is large enough. On it are a wand, incense (with charcoal if necessary), two white candles, a third candle (white, yellow, or red), a bowl of water, a symbol of earth (salt, sand, a rock or crystal, or a pentacle), matches, a crown of ivy or grain for the groom and a crown of flowers for the bride. The rings may also be there, traditionally on a wand, or the best man and maid of honor may carry them. Leaning against the altar is a broom, the old-fashioned round kind.

A white candle is put at each of the four directions (on tall stands or small tables) and two on the altar. If the wedding is outside and it is at all windy the candles will need to be protected by being put inside jars or glasses, unless outdoor candles or torches are used. These last two have long poles that can be decorated with ribbons and flowers. Putting matches at each candle will make lighting them go more smoothly. Alternatively, those who will need to use matches can carry them.

When everything is ready the officiants enter and stand behind the altar. A Priest and Priestess are required to ensure the blessing of both God and Goddess. After they enter, the officiants welcome everyone. This is also the time to explain to the guests what will happen. There will usually be non-Pagans there who will need to be put at ease. A printed program giving the text or at least an outline of the ritual will help. If the program gives enough detail it may be possible to eliminate the spoken explanation entirely, improving the flow of the ritual, but a welcome is still polite.

If the couple has a ritual for creating sacred space that they prefer they should use that, provided it does not establish the wall between the sacred and profane worlds (unless all the guests can fit into the circle). If they do not have one they wish to use, they can use the following one.

The people who are to serve as the representatives of the guardians of the elements go to their appropriate directions, where they stand outside the tables with the candles. Since water and earth are generally thought of as female and air and fire as male, the representatives are usually of the corresponding sex, although this is best left up to the couple. In the calling of the elements generally the Priest calls the male elements and the Priestess calls the female elements, but this is flexible also.

The elemental representatives may be part of the procession, in which case they will be with the bride and groom at this point. If so, they will be responsible for the invoking of the elements into themselves before the procession.

After explaining the ritual, the Priestess lights the two white candles on the altar to signify that sacred time has begun. (She may first sound a bell, gong, or drum.) She then goes about the circle with the wand, saying:

> *Blessed be this circle,*
> *a meeting place for the Gods and their people,*
> *a meeting place of love.*

If she does not generally use a wand, her hand will serve.

The Priest then lights the incense and brings it once around the circle, starting and stopping in the east. He holds it up and says:

> *Power of the East*
> *Power of Air*
> *Be with us here in this sacred place*
> *to bless the two who will come before you.*

He waves the incense over the representative of air and hands it to him or puts it on the table. (If the representatives of the elements are going to come in with the bride and groom, the Priest and Priestess will need to light the candles.) The representative lights the candle on the table. The Priest then goes to the altar and lights the white, yellow, or red candle. He brings it once around the circle, starting and stopping in the south. He holds it up and says:

> *Power of the South*
> *Power of Fire*
> *Be with us here in this sacred place*
> *to bless the two who will come before you.*

He moves the candle in a circle about the head of the representative of fire and then hands it to him or puts it on the table. The representative then lights the candle on the table. The Priest then goes to the altar and stands on its south side.

The Priestess or Priest then picks up the bowl of water from the altar and brings it once around the circle, starting and stopping in the west. She holds it up and says:

> *Powers of the West*
> *Powers of Water*
> *Be with us here in this sacred place*
> *to bless the two who will come before you.*

She sprinkles some on the representative of water and hands it to her or puts it on the table. The representative then lights the candle on the table. The Priestess then goes to the altar and picks up the symbol of earth. She brings it once around the circle, starting and stopping in the north. She holds it up and says:

> *Powers of the North*
> *Powers of Earth*
> *Be with us here in this sacred place*
> *to bless the two who will come before you.*

She holds it against the forehead of the representative of earth (if it is salt or sand, she may sprinkle some of it on her) and gives it to her or puts it on the table. The representative then lights the candle on the table. The Priestess then goes to the altar and stands on its north side.

The Priest stretches out his hands, palms up, and says:

> *Lady of Love,*
> *We ask your presence here*
> *to bless the two who will come before you.*

He drops his hands and the Priestess raises hers and says:

> *Lord of Love,*
> *We ask your presence here*
> *to bless the two who will come before you.*

She then drops her hands. If the couple prefer particular Goddess and God names, they can be used instead of "Lady and Lord of Love."

The Priest then goes to the north of the altar and stands beside the Priestess.

During the casting of the circle, the bride and groom will have been elsewhere. After the casting, someone previously chosen by them leaves the circle and goes to get them, or a drum, gong, bell, or horn may be sounded to call them.

The entrance may be as elaborate a processional as they wish. They may be preceded by someone with a torch, flowers, or the cup for the ritual, or ringing bells. They may come in with bridesmaids, ushers, and parents to music. Attendants are almost universal, and it is only natural to want friends with you on a journey of this sort. Or they may come in alone. The only requirement is that they not be touching. This is because of the ritual and psychological principle that deliberate abstention from something increases its effectiveness when it is finally achieved. They are not joined together yet. If they come with their parents, they say goodbye to them at the northeast of the circle and the parents go to where they will sit or stand for the rest of the ritual, and the bride and groom turn to face the circle.

From inside the circle the Priest and Priestess challenge the couple, saying:

Who comes before us?

Each answers by name. They are challenged again:

Why do you come before us today?

Each answers:

I wish to become one with (name).

They are challenged again:

What do you offer to each other as token?

They answer:

> *Perfect love and perfect trust.*

The challengers say:

> *All who bring such are doubly welcome.*

(This challenge is based on the first degree initiation ritual of Gardnerian Wicca).

After the challenge, the couple is greeted with kisses from the officiants and brought into the circle. They are brought to each quarter in turn. At the east the representative of air says:

> *The blessing of Air be upon this couple.*
> *Air is the quick change, hard to catch,*
> *The wind that blows through life.*
> *Throw yourself onto it, and let it bear you up.*

He moves the incense or waves it with a paper fan or feather so that the smoke touches the couple.

At the south, the representative of fire says:

> *The blessing of Fire be upon this couple.*
> *Fire burns away all that is impure.*
> *It is the passion that drew you together*
> *and the hearth flame that will keep*
> *   your home happy.*

He brings the candle close enough to the couple that they can feel its heat and then returns it to the table.

At the west, the representative of water says:

> *The blessing of Water be upon this couple.*
> *Water is the womb, the essence of life.*
> *It is the slow change, gracefully dancing.*
> *Rest in its flow, and let it hold you.*

She sprinkles them with the water.

At the north, the representative of earth says:

The blessing of Earth be upon this couple.
Earth is stability, solidity, existence.
It is cold and dark and empty.
But out of darkness, comes light
Out of cold, comes life
Out of the empty days, comes love
And out of these three, comes happiness.

She touches the symbol of earth to the foreheads of each.

The bride and groom are then turned to face away from each other, standing in the north with the bride facing west. The Priestess stands in front of the groom and the Priest in front of the bride. The bride and groom are each given a cup of wine while the Priest or Priestess says:

Wine is ecstasy, a path of magic,
the way to the Gods, a sign of life.

After drinking, the bride and groom both kneel. The Priest and Priestess bless them, stretching their arms over them while speaking. The Priestess says:

Gentle Goddess, attest the betrothal of
these young hearts

The Priest says:

Mighty God, attest the betrothal of
these young hearts.

The Priestess says:

Ever-Changing Moon, attest the betrothal of
these young hearts.

The Priest says:

Unconquered Sun, attest the betrothal of
these young hearts.

The Priestess says:

> *Land and Sea, attest the betrothal of*
> *these young hearts.*

The Priest says:

> *Air and Void, attest the betrothal of*
> *these young hearts.*

The Priestess says:

> *May all who are witnesses here ...*

The Priest says:

> *And all who may encounter them ...*

They both say:

> *Attest the betrothal of these young hearts.*

Instead of the Priest and Priestess saying all of each blessing, the "attest the betrothal of these young hearts" (which is from the Alexandrian Book of Shadows) can be said as a response by the other people there.

The broom is used by one of the officiants to sweep away all impurities and bad luck from the bride and groom. It is then placed on the ground behind them.

The Priestess then crowns the groom and the Priest crowns the bride. If they are wearing robes that open in the front these are then opened to anoint them. This should be done as discreetly as possible if non-Pagans are present. The couple stands and the Priest anoints the bride and the Priestess the groom with oil on the feet, knees, genitals, breasts, and lips. The robes are closed again after the anointing. If the anointing cannot be done, the Priest and Priestess may simply hold their hands in blessing over the same spots. These are the sacred spots of the body in Wicca—the feet which walk the path and are a symbol of power in many religions, the knees which kneel before the gods, the genitals which give life and pleasure, the breasts which give nourishment to the next generation, and the lips which will soon speak the vows. The anointing prepares the couple for what comes next—their consecration as Goddess and God.

After the anointing, the Priest and Priestess kneel. The Priest then says:

> *You are She, the One without beginning.*
> *You are the Mother of All,*
>   *Who gives birth to the world.*
> *You are the Essence,*
>   *from Whom all things are formed:*
> *Wherever we may look, You will be there.*
> *You are She of many names:*
> *When Your true face is known, all naming ceases.*
> *In Your presence all stop to wonder:*
> *All life is a prayer to You.*

The Priestess says:

> *You are He, dying and rising again and again.*
> *You are the Father of All, born in every moment.*
> *You are Existence, the Form shown by all things.*
> *Wherever we may look, You will be there.*
> *You are He of many names:*
> *though we lift your mask,*
> *there is no end to the naming.*
> *In Your presence all stop to wonder:*
> *All life is a prayer to you.*

The Priest and Priestess stand and the bride and groom are given the rings. They turn to face each other, take each others' hands, and say in turn:

> *I take you to my hand*
> *at the rising of the moon*
> *the setting of the stars*
> *to love and to honor*
> *through all that may come,*
> *through all our life together.*

(From "I take" to "the stars" is from the Alexandrian Book of Shadows.) As they say these words they put the rings on each others' hands. If they wish to make a further commitment, they say:

> *In all our lives,*
> *May we be reborn in the same time*
> > *and at the same place*
> > *that we may meet, and know, and remember,*
> > *and love again.*

(The last two lines are from the Gardnerian Book of Shadows.)

The bride then pours water into a cup and offers it to the groom. He drinks, pours more in and offers it to her. She drinks. This is the third drink. First was milk, the food of babies. Then was wine, food of gods and drunk by adults. Now both of those have been transcended by going to their common nature, pure liquidity. This is the ultimate invocation of Dionysus.

The cup used in the wedding is to be the emblem of the couple's life together, and so it must be new. After the wedding it is kept by the couple. It may be passed around at family rituals and used to drink toasts to the ancestors. If, gods forbid, the marriage should end in divorce, it will be needed for the ritual of parting. For this reason it should be breakable, and also to symbolize that the marriage formed in the wedding must be guarded if it is to stay whole.

After putting the water and cup back on the altar the bride and groom kiss, turn, and jump over the broom. This is a Gypsy custom that probably was picked up by them in Germany and the Netherlands and has now made its way into Neo-Paganism. Music starts, and people leave for the party.

Between the ritual and the party, the new couple should spend some time alone together. During this time the bride may wish to follow an old custom and put her hair up. This custom, found especially among the Celts, is based on the connection between marital status and hair style found in many peoples, among them Romans, Slavs, and Jews. By putting up her hair, the bride is marking the transition from the free state of the maiden to the state of the matron, with all its attendant responsibilities.

One of the most practiced wedding customs in modern America is the groom carrying the bride over the threshold. This is a

Pagan tradition, from the Romans. Since a Roman wife moved into her husband's house, her entry was an important event. To stumble on the threshold would insult the gods of her new household. Carrying her over it prevented this.

If this custom is objected to as patrifocal, the threshold guardians of the couple's home must still be honored. Entering into a house after marriage to set up a new household is a sacred act. It is the proper time to perform the house blessing ritual. (See Chapter 3.) Even if the couple has been living together, a new household has been established with the marriage and must be recognized ritually.

The establishment of a new household will require acquisition of family guardians. (The ritual for this is given in Chapter 3.) Articles for the shrine such as candles and offering bowls are a good choice for wedding presents from the parents of the couple. Especially appropriate would be for the parents of the bride to give a statue of a female guardian and the groom's family to give a statue of a male guardian. If the bride and groom wish to make their own guardian symbols, the materials could be given instead.

The traditional year and a day requirement can be met in two ways. First, the betrothal can last that long, with the wedding being the confirming event. Alternatively, the wedding can be the beginning of the period. In this case, the tying of the hands ceremony should take place at the wedding before the rings are exchanged. The Priest or Priestess would say the words. The part starting "Take this time of binding" would not be said, of course.

If the year and a day period starts at the wedding, the end of the period should be observed with a ritual and a party. It should be attended at least by the Priest and Priestess and the two legal witnesses of the wedding. The ritual can be a simple declaration by the couple that the marriage will continue, and then on to the party.

A word about names is in order. There are a number of choices of names a married couple might make. They can keep their previous names, take the husband's name, take the wife's name, take a name new to both, combine pieces of each name, or hyphenate their names, with either the wife's or husband's name first. The choice is up to the couple, as there is no obviously Neo-Pagan answer. I think it is important that a family have one name on which to hang their identity. Still, the people of Iceland (where all members of the family may have different names) would disagree.

The question hyphenators are most often asked is "What happens when your child marries, especially if she marries someone who also has a hyphenated name?" (I've heard the question many times myself; my legal name is hyphenated.) There is a simple solution. The wife keeps her mother's name and the husband keeps his father's, and the two are hyphenated to form a new family name unique to this couple. The result is men carrying on the male name and women carrying on the female name. By doing this the masculine is honored by the man and the feminine is honored by the woman. Alternatively, the names could cross in each generation, with women carrying on their father's name and men carrying on their mother's. Either way will honor both female and male, and that is something which is very consistent with the ideals of Neo-Paganism.

Parting

Divorce should never be easy, and, people being what they are, it never is. A ritual to mark it, however, might ease it some, while at the same time concentrating its effect. And since a marriage is begun with a ritual, is should end with one as well—a divorce is as sacred an act as a wedding. Such rituals have been lacking in most religious communities, but Pagans have made an effort to develop them.

Just as a wedding is not solely a personal act, neither is a parting. If a couple has children this is obvious. Every effort must be made to minimize problems the breakup of the marriage may cause them. Our Mother and Father expect no less.

It is not so obvious, perhaps, that a divorce affects the community. But as a community is affected by the marriages within it, it is also affected by the divorces. If the community is called upon to witness a wedding, it should be called upon to witness a parting. This is not to suggest that a large party be gathered, with a sit down dinner and dance. But there are people who were important in the wedding who deserve a part in its dissolution.

Now, divorces are not always friendly, and this ritual may not always be possible. But if both husband and wife are Pagans they owe it to themselves and to their community to make the effort. Through it, healing may come to all. At least it can begin.

Perform this ritual after the legal portion of the divorce is final. This should be the last act in the divorce, marking its completion.

Gather together the Priest and Priestess who presided at the wedding, as well as the two witnesses that the law required. The witnesses stand in for the community. If the same two people cannot attend, choose a man and a woman, either both acceptable to both members of the couple or one acceptable to each.

Because the ritual involves planting seeds it should be done outdoors. Even in a city some appropriate spot may be found—a secluded corner of a park, a vacant lot, even a roadside if necessary. Since the spot may acquire painful associations as a result of the ritual, a trip to a place which will not be encountered regularly by the couple is worth the effort. If it absolutely cannot be performed outdoors, choose a location that is neutral. Strong feelings may well be released during the ritual, so the location needs to be one where both members of the couple feel at home, or at least where they feel equally not at home.

Ritual

On a small table put a cord of natural fibers. This should be the cord used in the betrothal or wedding if it is available. (For an inside ritual, use thread or string instead of rope.) You will also need a knife, a cup filled with water, and some seeds. If at all possible, the cup should be the one from which the couple drank at their wedding. Whatever cup is used, it must be breakable. Two rocks or hammers will be needed to break it with. Prepare a small hole in the ground, leaving the spade next to it. (If the ritual is being performed indoors, you will need a lunch size paper bag half-filled with dirt and additional dirt to fill it the rest of the way.) If you wish to call sacred space according to your tradition, you may do so.

The husband and wife say to those there:

> You who stood with us at the beginning of
>   this marriage:
> We have asked you to be here at its end
>   that you might see that it is done rightly.

The Priest or Priestess tie the couple's wrists together with the cord. (If the couple is not friendly enough for both to be there, or if one of them is unavailable for any other reason, tie the person present to a picture of the one who is not there.) The presiding officer who does not do the tying says:

> *The ties that bound you were strong ...*

One then cuts the cord with the knife while the other says:

> *But even the strongest ties break ...*

The one who cut it holds up the cord and the other says:

> *Leaving their echoes behind.*

The couple then put the cord in the ground, saying as they do:

> *May the ties dissolve ...*

They then put some dirt on top of the cord and plant the seeds (this is especially important if the couple have children), saying:

> *Nourishing what they have produced.*

The Priest or Priestess offers them the cup of water, saying:

> *This cup that once bound you*
> *now dissolves the binding.*

Or, if it is not the original cup:

> *A cup once bound you,*
> *A cup now dissolves the binding.*

They each take a drink from the cup, pouring the remaining water on the seeds. Then they both break the cup and put the pieces in the ground, saying:

> *No more will it bind*
> *No more will it unbind.*

They fill in the hole and stamp the dirt down. (If a bag is used, they pack it with their hands.) The Priest and Priestess hold their hands out in blessing and say:

Go now, walk freely
from this place of unbinding.

The couple walk away in different directions without looking back, while the Priest or Priestess says:

Untie, untie
the bonds of fate
and loose the knots
that held you together.
Dissolve
Dissipate
Disappear
They pass away slowly
until nothing is left
but the shape of where they once were
ready to be filled again.

If a bag has been used, the Priest or Priestess will need to bury it outside later.

❧ 11 ❧

Death

What happens when a Pagan dies? We have been so identified with the material and so attached to the Earth. Now what?

Pagans believe in a spiritual aspect of the person, a soul or a spirit. Their beliefs about this differ, but they mostly agree on its existence. And while it is obviously connected to and affected by a material body, it survives that material body's demise.

Where does it go? Most Pagans would agree that it goes to another world, variously called the Summerland, Tir na nOg, the Land of Faerie, or simply the Otherworld. The image most often employed is of a water or air journey, either to the north, the direction of greatest darkness, or to the west, where the sun dies his daily death. The soul goes to be rested and refreshed, to relax from this world's trials and assimilate this world's lessons. It may stay in this land for a long or a short time, and the Summerland's time may run at a different speed than ours anyway.

When ready, the soul is reborn into this world. This is our world: we live within it, we die within it, and we return to it. There may be another world between our lives, but we return to live again. Most Pagans would agree that we are reborn into a human body, though some may accept the possibility of animal rebirth.

There are two theories of how the circumstances of rebirth are determined. One is that the soul itself decides, based on what it feels it most needs to continue its advancement towards godhood. The more common belief is that one's actions in this life determine the circumstances of the next life, that cause and effect operate across the borders of death. Neo-Pagans have borrowed the Hindu word "karma" to express this. By a soul's karma it is returned to enter a body, at conception (say those who believe human life starts then) or later (say those who don't).

It is possible that we are reborn elsewhere, on other physical planets or spiritual planes. As a Pagan, though, I am most likely to be reborn on this world, my beloved Earth. Where does a Pagan go when he dies? There is really no need for him to go anywhere.

Sometimes a soul does not accept its death, does not even believe it *has* died. This is most common with sudden deaths. Then instead of being able to relax in the Summerland while preparing for rebirth, the soul tries to come back. In short, it becomes a ghost. Dealing with such ghosts consists mainly of convincing them of their death. One of the purposes of Pagan death customs (wake, funeral, commemoration, and Samhain) is to acknowledge the death and thereby convince the dead person of it.

That there are apparently conflicting beliefs regarding death is natural. For instance, the Romans, while believing that the dead had gone to another world, still performed rituals that implied that the dead lived on in the tomb. This phenomenon is not limited to ancient times. I once heard the Christian parents of a murdered man say they were going to the cemetery to tell their son the news that his murderer had been convicted. Reincarnation, the Summerland, grave rituals, ancestor rites—these are all aspects of the complicated pattern of Paganism. They help both the living and the dead, and that is enough to justify them.

Paganism does not have the same kind of comforting words as some other religions. We cannot tell ourselves that our loved ones are now living forever in a better place, or that we will see them again when we ourselves die.

We have our own ways of comfort. We have experienced death and rebirth many times. We have followed the seasons, watching life return in the spring. We have faced death at Samhain, welcoming our ancestors and honoring death itself.

Death and rebirth, survival after death and return, are not just beliefs to us. We know them like we know our own height. They are part of our lives; not something to be thought of at funerals, but guides for everyday living.

We belong to this world, and we will return here. We belong to our loved ones, and we will return with them. This is how Pagans comfort each other in the face of loss, with the ease born of familiarity and the knowledge born of experience.

Wake

"Wake" means "watch." It came from the custom of watching over a dead person. This may have had the mundane purpose of protecting him from robbers or other predators, but it is more likely to have been to protect him from bad spirits or to prevent his spirit from bothering the living.

The way the wake has evolved in our country is for family and friends to gather in a room in a funeral home. The deceased is there in his casket, and people stand around wondering what they're supposed to do. At some point there is a prayer service. Finally everyone talks to each other about anything, as long as it has nothing to do with the business at hand. The whole event seems orchestrated for the purpose of denying that a death has occurred.

This way of holding a wake is not all bad. It reminds us that even in the midst of death life goes on. It emphasizes the ties of family and friends in a time of crisis. But it leaves out what should be an important part of the event. Before we can reassure ourselves that life goes on, we need first to recognize that someone has died and then remember that person.

A funeral should be formal and ritualistic. Formality is very comforting. When everything is falling apart, structure is welcome. No one in the midst of grief should be expected to organize a ritual or develop meaningful ways of expressing his grief.

The wake should be less formal. Different people have different needs, and those who need an informal gathering should be given one. Remember, too, that a person's death affects those who are outside of the Pagan community. It is common for a funeral to be limited to those very close to the dead person, but for a wake to be attended by a large number of acquaintances, including coworkers and sometimes even friends of friends. These people need to grieve in their own way. Schedule time for both the usual mingling and a remembrance service.

The wake as Americans know it is not held in all cultures. In England, for example, the viewing of the body is not held. Some people think the viewing is macabre, while others find in it a way of convincing themselves that their friend is really dead. A wake can be held with the casket open, or the casket closed, or no casket at all. None of this is essentially Pagan, although the visible presence of the corpse is indicative of the easy relationship with death and the world cultivated by Pagans. If the casket is not there, a picture of the dead person should be used as the focal point for the wake. However, there must be no attempt to deny the fact of death. One of the purposes of the wake and the funeral is to start the process of accepting loss.

Since a death affects an entire family it will naturally affect the children of the family. They should take part in the wake and the funeral to the extent that they wish to. If they do not feel up to participating, that is fine. If they want to take part, however, they should not be prevented. It is a sign of maturity to take part; by doing so they are entering into the responsibilities of life, one of which is an acknowledgement of death.

If possible, hold the wake in the home of the deceased. The household guardians and the spirits of the ancestors will be able to take part more easily if the ritual is on their home turf. From a practical point of view, this will preclude problems with what you choose to do, as well as conveying a message that death is a part of normal life, not something to be quarantined.

If it is not possible to have the wake at home, make sure that what will be done is possible in the funeral home. The further in advance that arrangements can be made, the better. If the director is concerned that noises will disturb other wakes, perhaps a non-conflicting time or another funeral home can be found.

Ritual

After sufficient time has passed to allow for informal socializing, the person who is presiding calls for attention, with a drum or bells. He then says:

> *We are here to remember one of us who has died.*
> *Everyone is part of many communities*
> *and those of* (name) *are here today.*
> *It is time to remember* (name).
> *When the talking stick reaches you,*
> *tell us about* (name).
> *Speak from your heart of what you most know.*
> *If you do not wish to speak,*
> *pass the stick on.*
> *There is no shame in not speaking,*
> *only in not remembering.*

Pass a talking stick. This is a short stick, decorated if you wish, that is passed from hand to hand. The holder of the stick speaks of the dead for as long as she wishes, trying always to speak from the heart. When she is finished she passes it to the next person. While the stick is in someone's possession, she may not be interrupted.

When the stick reaches the presiding official again, he says:

> *We have gathered and we have remembered.*
> *We have done the right thing.*
> *It is good.*

The others say:

> *It is good.*

The presiding official puts the stick on or in the coffin and says:

> *Our thoughts go with you.*
> *We will remember.*

He then thanks everyone for coming and invites them to stay for a while. This will be a good time for more socializing or more ritual, as may seem right. If it is possible, there may be drumming.

Funeral

There is no obviously Pagan way to dispose of a dead person. Pagans have practiced cremation, burial, and exposure. Their dead have been laid to rest in stone tombs, the earth, ponds, and pyramids. Bodies have been left permanently interred, rearranged after the flesh has rotted, and removed to make room for new bodies. Any way a body can be disposed of, Pagans have done. We cannot look strictly to our past for guidance. Instead we must ask ourselves how a Pagan's body should be disposed of today.

The two choices for disposal of remains in our culture are burial and cremation. Neither are particularly acceptable from an environmental point of view. The way bodies are usually buried prevents them from returning to the soil and the intense heat used in crematoria (supplied by polluting sources) leaves very little that the earth can use. Perhaps someday Pagans will have cemeteries where the dead can be buried with minimum packaging, allowing a true return to the soil.

In the meantime we still have to do something. Both ways have a long history of Pagan use behind them, but there is nothing particularly Pagan or non-Pagan about either of them. It comes down to personal choice, then.

In any case, a Pagan will want to rest gently in the Earth, and not make his death one more scar upon her lovely face. No large memorial, no bronze casket, preferably no embalming. At best, just a body, with such ritual tools and personal items that should belong to no one else. Second best, a wooden box that will soon return the body's elements to the soil. And if he is cremated, then the ashes should be returned to the earth from which they came.

Two rituals are given here, one for those whose path is Wicca, and one for those who practice shamanism. Because of its elaborate symbolism, the first is best for a funeral attended mostly by Pagans.

Ritual 1

This is a descent with the dead to the Land of the Dead, with a final farewell there and an affirmation of rebirth. This is followed by a return to the world of the living. The Land of the Dead is conceived of here as a shadow realm, in many ways a mirror image of this world. Thus the dark clothing and white faces and doing every-thing widdershins (counterclockwise). This is not to say, of course, that the Otherworld is a depressing place. The entry of the living in this rite, however, is only into its outer region, its vestibule, and that is indeed a forbidding place, especially for the living.

This is a formal, highly ritualistic event. That is good for impressing on all that a death has occurred and that they are dealing with it. If a mourner has experienced the same form of funeral numerous times, she has the added advantage of not having to think too much at a difficult time. She can run on automatic, as it were.

The ritual is performed at the cemetery or crematorium. The grave should be laid out so that the foot end is in the north or west, if possible. At the head end of the grave put two chairs on either side of an altar. On the altar put a knife, a cup of water, a plate with three apple seeds, and a bowl of ocher or other red powder. If the dead person had ancestral symbols in his shrine, place them on or behind the altar. Put a bowl of white powder (chalk or flour) at the edge of the sacred space, next to a large bowl or bottle of water, a towel, and a plate with bread or crackers on it.

Before the body is brought to the cemetery or crematorium the Priest and Priestess go there and create sacred space. They will need an assistant who will serve as Guide of Souls. He will also hand required objects to the participants of the ritual. For the actual creat-ing of sacred space they do everything widdershins (counterclock-wise, the direction of death and dissolution). They wear black robes. They call on the gods and goddesses of death. The Priestess says:

> *Come, Dark Mother,*
> *Come to us,*
> *Out of the night*
> *on owl's wings.*
> *Come, by the screeching wind.*
> *Come, by the cleansing fire.*
> *Come, by the absorbing water.*
> *Come, by the restful earth.*
> *Come, by the Spirit that waits.*
> *Come to Your people.*
> *Be with us now.*

The Priest will say:

> *We call upon the Horned One,*
> *The Stern Lord of the Land of Death.*
> *Come, by the whirlwind.*
> *Come, by the force of fire.*
> *Come, by the receiving sea.*
> *Come, by the accepting earth.*
> *Come, by the Spirit that waits.*
> *Come to Your people.*
> *Be with us now.*

They then sit in silence while the assistant goes to summon the others. Either the Priest or the Priestess may start a slow drumbeat to call the dead person home.

The others are also dressed in black or other dark colors. When they are brought to the place they come widdershins and in a spiral if possible.

The nearest relative (or friend if she has no relatives) of the opposite sex to the deceased has a cord tied around his wrist, with the other end tied to the coffin.

When they reach the edge of the sacred place the assistant says:

> *We are at the edge of the Land of Death.*
> *Will you go on?*

The relative says:

> *We will go on,*
> *with steadfast hearts.*

The others say:

> *We will go on.*

As the people cross the border into the sacred space, the assistant whitens their faces. With a large number of people, there may need to be more than one person doing this, or the whitening can be reduced to a line across the forehead. Unless there is an exceptional amount of room the coffin will have to be brought to its place by the shortest route, but the others are brought in a widdershins spiral towards the center. As they go, the assistant says:

> *We spiral down*
> *into the center.*
> *We have left the land of the living behind.*

A journey of seven circuits will bring to mind the ancient Mediterranean belief of the journey of the soul through the seven planets. If there isn't enough room for seven, try to make three, to bring to mind the sacredness of that number, number of the moon's phases and the sacred number of the Indo-Europeans. When everyone has stopped, the body is placed next to or over the grave. If there has been drumming, it stops. The relative is given a knife by the Priest and he cuts the cord, saying:

> *Everything changes*
> *Everything passes.*
> *Go, friend, on your journey.*
> *We have come this far in love*
> *but we can no longer walk with you.*
> *Change may not be undone;*
> *that which passes, passes away.*
> *Go, now, to the Land of the Gods,*
> *the Summerland, the Land of Apples,*
> *there to rest and be refreshed.*
> *But when you are ready*
> *and reborn on the earth,*
> *may it be in the same time and the same place*
> *as your loved ones*
> *that we may meet, and know, and remember,*
> *and love again.*

(From "may it be" to the end is from the Gardnerian Book of Shadows.)

If the relative is unable to say this, perfectly understandable under the circumstances, it may be said by the Priest or Priestess, whichever is the same sex as the relative. The Priestess then takes the ocher from the altar and uses it to draw a sacred sign that meant much to the deceased (a pentagram, Thor's hammer, circle, etc.) on her forehead, saying:

Receive rebirth from my hand
when it is time
when it is time.

The relative says:

Go now, marked with the sign of life,
on the way that has been taken
by so many before you.

The cord is put in the coffin and it is closed. If it is to be buried, the coffin is lowered into the ground while the Priestess says:

We commit (here all the names by which
she was known, include nicknames
and craft names) *to your care.*
Love her, cherish her, feed her,
Let her grow
until she is ready for rebirth.

If the relative is a woman she now pours water on the coffin. If not, another woman will be chosen to do it. She will say:

The sea is the womb
from which we sprang
and which absorbs us again in the end.

A man (the relative if a man or someone else if not) drops three apple seeds onto the coffin. He says:

The seed goes into the darkness
and from it comes new life.

If the deceased is to be cremated, this is the point where it will be done and where "We commit, etc." will be said.

If the deceased is being buried, the close relatives and friends help fill in the grave. It need not all be done now, but each person should put in at least one handful of dirt. Although painful, this is a healing act, providing one last gift for their loved one while at the same time impressing on them the finality of their loss.

When this is done, the Priest says:

> *She is with the ancestors now,*
> *in the Land of Youth.*

The Priestess says:

> *This very moment,*
> *even as we stand here in the Land of Death,*
> *new life is being born.*
> *Perhaps even our friend is ready to be reborn.*
> *Out there, in the world you live in,*
> *life goes on.*
> *Life is good.*
> *Blessed be life!*

All say:

> *Blessed be life!*

They then spiral out again, deosil this time. It is important that they turn the same number of times they did coming in. As they leave the circle the assistant or others wipes away the white from their faces. When they are all out they turn to face the center once more. The relative or someone else says:

> *You have gone to be with the Ancestors*
> *and we will remember you.*

All:

> *We will remember you.*

Relative:

> *On the day of remembering*
> *and all the days between …*

All:

We will remember you.

Relative:

When the ocean brings us words
and the wind whispers its messages ...

All:

We will remember you.

Relative:

At the rising of the moon
At the coming of the sun ...

All:

We will remember you.

Relative:

In the lives we live
and the ways we go ...

All:

We will remember you.

Relative:

Have no doubt
Feel no fears ...

All:

We will remember you.

Everyone is given something to eat from the plate of bread or crackers, to mark the return to the land of the living. They then go to change their clothes before gathering somewhere to eat and drink and talk. After the others have left, the Priest and Priestess recast the sacred space, this time deosil before saying farewell to the gods and banishing it.

Ritual 2

This is performed at the gravesite, or at the spot where the ashes will be disposed of. A pile of stones is next to the grave. One will be needed for each person there. Depending on cemetery require-ments, these can be small or large. If the cemetery won't allow stones at all, perhaps they will allow pegs that can be pushed into the ground. If even pegs are unacceptable, a container of birdseed from which each person can take a handful may be used. There are drums for those who will wish them. The dead person's drum is put into the grave by his nearest relative so that the coffin will be on top of it. In this way, the dead person might ride his drum to the land of the gods. The coffin is lowered and the hole partially filled. There is slow drumming while this is done.

The drumming continues while whoever is presiding says:

> *Our friend is dead.*
> *He is gone.*
> *Our friend has set sail.*
> *He is on his way.*
> *Go, with our blessings.*
> *Our drums fill your sails*
> *and speed you home*
> *to the Summerland,*
> *the Land of Apples.*
> *Go, and rest.*
> *And when rested, return.*
> *Be reborn among friends.*
> *Be reborn among your people.*

The nearest relative then throws some apple seeds into the grave. Each person then picks up a marker (stone, peg, or handful of birdseed) and lays it down around the grave so that together they form the shape of a ship. This is also the shape of a vagina. Thus the ship that carries the dead person away is also the path through which he will be reborn.

The people can lay the stones down in silence or say a good-bye as they do so. It must be understood by all that the choice of silence or words is theirs. If they would like to say something, but don't know what, they can say:

> One last thing I do for you
> as you go on your way.

Or simply:

> Goodbye.

When all the stones are placed, the person presiding says:

> Goodbye, goodbye.
> Go on your way.
> You go your way, and we go ours.
> We will remember you.

The others repeat "We will remember you," and then they leave the cemetery without looking back.

After either ritual everyone goes to someone's house to socialize further. The living have their own needs.

If you have a stove with a pilot light, it would be in keeping with tradition to put it out before leaving home. (Remember to shut off the gas!) Then relight it when you return after the funeral.

Be sure to call out the deceased's name at the next Samhain.

Commemoration

There is a custom among some peoples, particularly well-known among Jews, of commemorating the anniversary of a relative's death. The Yiddish for it is "Yahrzeit," the "Year-time." It fulfills several functions. One of the more important is to allow for a socially sanctioned time of mourning that has a distinct end.

Although mourning is a personal thing and the necessary length varies from person to person, sometimes people feel guilty about stopping it. An official day on which it is OK to stop is a great help to such people.

Among Pagans, commemorations are frequently held a year and a day after the event. This allows for a whole year before starting a new phase. The commemoration therefore acknowledges that a period of change is over and a new one is beginning.

At the beginning of the commemoration, light a candle which will burn for the whole period (Yahrzeit candles, candles in a jar which burn for a long time, can be found in many grocery stores), while saying:

> *You are with us now.*
> *We have not forgotten you.*

The day is spent in fasting, meditation, and remembering. Friends may wish to stop by and remember with the close relatives. At the very end of the day, visit the cemetery. Perform the acts of remembrance performed at Samhain and leave without looking back.

Alternatively, if people consider that their mourning has reached an appropriate point by the Samhain after the funeral, these observances could be held then. Whenever they are held, though, make sure you remember your relative at Samhain. It is especially important to call out their name at the first Samhain after death. Remember them.

Afterword

Children are born to the People. We welcome them and bless them, teach them, celebrate with them. When they come of age we honor them and send them on their way with our blessings, to find lives of their own and continue the work. And then we ourselves someday die, leaving them behind in our place.

It is good that things should be this way. We live, we raise children, we die. And we are reborn. And so the wheel turns. It is indeed good. The world is indeed good, and all its ways are good. We who call ourselves Pagans say this, that the world is good.

May our children be blessed. May our children bless us. May all who read these words be blessed, and may you pass this blessing on and on, handing the old ways down, for as long as earth and sky endure.

Protective Symbols

These can be painted or carved over doors and windows, or drawn on them with oil or water during house blessings. They may also be painted, carved, or burned on pieces of wood and worn around the neck as amulets, or drawn on someone's forehead with a finger, either plain or with oil or water as part of a blessing. Finally, they can be painted or carved on a crib to extend protection over a baby.

Symbol	How Made	Meaning
		Pentagram—the four elements, plus spirit, bound together.

Symbol	How Made	Meaning
		Moon—invokes the protection of the Goddess.
		Three dots—the Triple Goddess.
		Pillar—the God, the Cosmic Pillar.
		Equal-armed cross—the four directions, the elements, sky and earth, the sacred and the profane. Used by both Pagans and Christians, and thus especially useful in inter-faith families.
		Thor's hammer—symbol of the great Norse protector of the common people.
		Circle—wholeness and completeness, and thus a barrier against external forces.

Symbol	How Made	Meaning
		Twin-bladed axe—both a Goddess symbol and a God symbol. Called a "labrys" when used as a Goddess symbol, it is one of the common emblems of the supposed matriarchal culture of ancient Crete. It is also the typical weapon of the Indo-European thunder and warrior god.
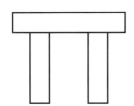	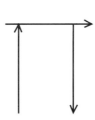	Dolmen— Neolithic portal between our world and the world of the gods. It therefore provides an opening for sacred influence and protection.

❧ APPENDIX 2 ❧

Table of Offerings

Different types of spiritual entities prefer different types of offerings. If you are working with a particular deity or spirit, you will need to research just what that deity prefers. This table, however, is a good start, especially when working with the unnamed spirits likely to be encountered.

	Food	Drink	Incense	Other
Nature Spirits	Cornmeal, bread, grain, fruit, cheese	Beer	Sage	Tobacco, quartz pebbles
House Spirits	Bread, salt, oil, fruit	Milk, wine, beer	Frankincense, rosemary	

	Food	Drink	Incense	Other
Border Guardian	Eggs, honey, cakes	Milk, wine, beer	Rosemary, thyme, juniper	Flower garlands
Hearth Guardian	Bread, butter, oil	Milk	Pine, rosemary	
Threshold Guardian	Barley, bread	Wine	Juniper	
Garden Spirits	Bread, fruit, honey, cornmeal	Water, mead, milk	Bay	Flowers
Deities in General	Bread	Wine, beer, milk	Frankincense	
Birth Goddesses	Bread, eggs, cookies	Milk, breast milk	Sandalwood, mint, rose	Infant's hair, umbilical cord
Ancestor Spirits	Beans, food and drink from the family table		Caraway	Hair

APPENDIX 3

Colors for Occasions

Samhain	Black
Yule	Red, green, white, gold
Imbolc	Red, green
Ostara	Yellow, pastels
May Day	Green, multicolored
Midsummers	Yellow, rainbow
Lammas	Gold
Harvest	Yellow, orange, red, purple (colors of fall leaves and twilight)
Full or waxing moon	White, silver, light blue
Dark moon	Black, dark blue

Glossary

ASPERGILL: An instrument used to sprinkle consecrated water.

ATHAME: A black-hilted knife used by Wiccans in rituals. It represents fire, air, or spirit, and is used primarily as a means of projecting the Wiccan's will.

CEREMONIAL MAGIC: A system of magic that uses intricate rituals to effect either material or spiritual results. Most (but not all) forms of ceremonial magic are heavily influenced by medieval Jewish mysticism.

CERNUNNOS: Celtic god depicted with stag's antlers, a ram-headed snake, and a torque (neck-ring of twisted metal). The most common name for the Wiccan God, most likely meaning "horned."

CHARGE: A piece of Wiccan scripture in the form of a declaration by the Goddess to her children. Composed by Doreen Valiente and Gerald Gardner from a variety of sources.

CIRCLE: A consecrated area in which many Neo-Pagan rituals take place. In Wicca it is considered to be an in-between place, neither in the sacred nor the mundane worlds.

CIRCLE-CASTING: The ritual by which a circle (q.v.) is constructed.

COVEN: A small group of Wiccans who practice Wicca together.

DAGDA: Irish god. His name means "the good god," a reference to ability rather than morality. He may be equivalent to Cernunnos.

DEMETER: Greek goddess of vegetation, especially grain. The second half of her name definitely means "mother"; the first half *may* mean "earth." Equivalent to the Roman Ceres, from which we get the word "cereal."

DEOSIL: Gaelic term for clockwise. This direction is used by Pagans for most ritual acts.

DIONYSUS: Greco-Roman god of wine, intoxication, ecstasy, and faithful marriage.

DISCORDIANISM: A semi-serious Neo-Pagan (sort of) religion which worships (but does not necessarily believe in) Discordia, goddess of chaos.

DUALISM: A philosophical outlook which divides phenomena into two opposing categories. The possible ways of doing this are limitless. Popular ones include spiritual/material (metaphysical dualism), good/evil (ethical dualism), or male/female (sexual dualism).

ELEMENT: One of the four (sometimes five) modes of existence. The elements are air, fire, water, and earth (often spirit).

GOD'S EYE: A decoration made from two crossed sticks entwined with yarn. May be used as ancestral images, elemental emblems, or seasonal decorations.

GROVE: Term used by some Neo-Pagans for a small group which practices rituals together.

GUARDIANS: 1. Spirits that watch over a place or group of people. 2. Adults appointed by parents as guides for their children. 3. Spirits that rule the four directions (in this sense usually called "Guardians of the Watchtowers").

GUIDED MEDITATION: An imagined journey to a sacred place or to encounter sacred beings which uses a text describing the journey. The text is read out loud and the journeyers imagine the journey based on it.

HANDFASTING: Originally a term for betrothal, it has become the Neo-Pagan term for a wedding.

HERMES: Greek god of travelers, merchants, commerce, and thieves. Equivalent to Roman Mercury.

ISIS: Egyptian mother goddess, invoked especially for protection. Her worship became popular in Rome, as well as among ceremonial magicians.

JANUS: Roman god of doorways and beginnings.

KAMIDANA: A Shinto god-shelf; the family shrine in a Shinto home.

KARMA: Literally meaning "action," this Hindu term has been adopted by Westerners to mean the accumulated effects of a person's actions, especially with regards to their influence on rebirth.

KWANZAA: African-American festival held from December 26th-January 1st. Celebrates the strengths of African-American culture.

LARES: Roman guardians of the home and family.

LIBATION: A liquid offering which is poured out to a spiritual being.

LITANY: A type of prayer which involves a leader and a group alternating lines.

LUGH: Irish craftsman god. The most widely worshiped of the Celtic gods. Equivalent to Welsh Lleu and Gaulish Lugos.

MANANNAN MAC LIR: Gaelic god of the sea, particularly of the Irish sea. Connected also with horses, like so many sea deities. Under his Welsh form, Manawyddan, son of Llyr, he was the second husband of Rhiannon (q.v.).

MENORAH: Jewish candelabra of eight candles, used to celebrate Hanukkah, the Jewish midwinters holiday.

MEZUZAH: Small case containing verses from the Hebrew scriptures that is attached to the door frames of Orthodox and Conservative Jewish homes.

MITHRAS: Persian and Roman god of friendship, justice, and truth. Patron of a Roman Men's Mysteries cult. Also spelled "Mithra." Equivalent to Hindu Mitra.

NEO-PAGANISM: A modern religion based on a blending of ancient Paganism with new ideas.

NUMINOUS: Possessing sacred power.

PAGAN: A practitioner of any of the Pagan religions, either of the ancient world or the modern.

PALEO-PAGANISM: The polytheistic religions preceding and surviving Judaism, Buddhism, Christianity, and Islam. Generally thought of as referring to the religions of ancient Rome, Greece, Egypt, etc., it also includes some forms of Shinto, Vedic Hinduism, some of the surviving Native American traditions, and the native religions of Africa.

PENATES: Roman guardians of food storage. Frequently confused with the lares (q.v.).

PENTAGRAM: A five-pointed interwoven star, symbolizing the four elements plus spirit combining to form the world. (See Appendix 1 for illustration.)

PERSEPHONE: Greek goddess, queen of the land of the dead and daughter of Demeter (q.v.). Equivalent to the Roman Proserpine.

POWER ANIMAL: A shaman's guiding spirit, manifesting in animal form.

PUCA: Celtic nature spirit. Equivalent to Puck and possibly Robin Goodfellow.

RHIANNON: Character in Welsh legend who was most likely a goddess. Since her name means "Great Queen," and she is associated with horses, twins, and the sea, she was probably the Welsh version of the Indo-European goddess of sovereignty. Likely equivalent to the Irish Macha and possibly the Gaulish Epona.

SAINING: Common name for Neo-Pagan blessing of a child. The word was originally a Northern English variation of "signing," meaning "baptism."

SHAMAN: A traditional healer who effects his cures while travelling in his soul in a supernatural world. He is able to travel there by means of percussion and/or, less commonly, hallucinogenic plants.

SKYCLAD: Ritually nude.

THOR: Norse god of thunder, battle, protection, and rowdiness. Special protector of the simple folk.

THRESHOLD: The horizontal base of a doorway. A sacred spot, frequently the location of worship of household gods.

WAND: A length of wood of almost any size (although eighteen inches is common) used by Wiccans in rituals. It represents air or fire and is used primarily as a means of projecting the Wiccan's will.

WASSAIL: Spiced heated ale or cider drunk at Yule.

WHEEL OF THE YEAR: Term used by many Pagans to describe the seasonal holidays when seen as a whole.

WICCA: Neo-Pagan religion developed in the 1950s by Gerald Gardner, Doreen Valiente, and others. Originally composed of elements from British folklore and customs combined with ceremonial magic, it has undergone great changes in America in recent years due to an influx of feminist and Native American spirituality.

WIDDERSHINS: Counterclockwise.

WODEN: Old English god of travel, wisdom, justice, and magic. Equivalent to the Norse Odhinn and German Wotan.

ZEUS: Greek god of lightning, kingship, and justice. His name means "Shining One," or perhaps "Bright Sky." Equivalent to the Roman god Jupiter.

References and Resources

Books and Articles

Ashcroft-Nowicki, Dolores. *First Steps in Ritual*. Wellingborough, U.K.: The Aquarian Press, 1982. Ritual theory, with rituals for a variety of occasions. Includes a ritual for attracting a Slavic house-spirit and a Chinese ritual for honoring the god of the stove.

Austen, Hallie Inglehart. *The Heart of the Goddess*. Shaky scholarship, but contains wonderful images for shrines. Some rituals.

Bingham, Mindy, Judy Edmondson, and Sandy Stryker. *Choices: A Teen Woman's Journal for Self-Awareness and Personal Planning*. Santa Barbara, CA: Advocacy Press, 1985.

Bittleston, Adam. *The Sun Dances: Prayers and Blessings from the Gaelic*. Edinburgh: Floris Books, 1960. Excerpts from *Carmina Gadelica*. (See Carmichael, Alexander.)

Bly, Robert. *Iron John: A Book About Men*. Reading, MA: Addison-Wesley Publishing Company, 1990. Men's coming of age experiences as imaged in fairy tales.

Brand, John. *Observations on the Popular Antiquities of Great Britain*. New York: AMS Press, 1970. Originally published in 1848. A gold mine of information, it gives customs for seasonal celebrations, birth, handfasting, betrothal, funeral, and much more.

Brown, Judith. "A Cross-Cultural Study of Female Initiation Rites," *American Anthropologist* 65 1963, pp. 837-53.

Buckland, Raymond. *The Complete Book of Saxon Witchcraft*. New York: Samuel Weiser, 1974. Written for a coven, it includes seasonal rituals, handfasting, handparting, birth rite, and funeral.

Campanelli, Pauline. *Ancient Ways: Reclaiming Pagan Traditions*. St. Paul, MN: Llewellyn Publications, 1991.

_____ . *Wheel of the Year: Living the Magical Life*. St. Paul, MN: Llewellyn Publications, 1989. Both this book and *Ancient Ways* give folk traditions and rituals for seasonal observances. Both are excellent sources for family observances.

Carmichael, Alexander. *Carmina Gadelica*. 6 vols. Edinburgh: Oliver and Boyd, Ltd., 1940. Prayers and songs collected in the Hebrides around the turn of the century. Some made their way into the Gardnerian Book of Shadows. Magnificent. Hard to find, but worth the effort.

Carroll, David. *Spiritual Parenting*. New York: Paragon House, 1990. Advice on child rearing from a New Age point of view. Includes tips on teaching meditation to children.

The Circle of Life: Rituals from the Human Family Album. Ed. by David Cohen. San Francisco, CA: Harper, 1991. Photographs of rites of passage with explanations. Covers from birth to death.

Crowley, Aleister. *777 and Other Qabalistic Writings of Aleister Crowley*. Ed. by Israel Regardie. New York: Samuel Weiser, 1973. Contains lists of correspondences, organized by Sephiroth, planets, and elements. Mostly useful in this context for moon and sun.

Cunningham, Scott. *Cunningham's Encyclopedia of Magical Herbs*. St. Paul, MN: Llewellyn Publications, 1985.

_____ . *Wicca: A Guide for the Solitary Practitioner*. St. Paul, MN: Llewellyn Publications, 1988. Although concerned mainly with those who work alone, many of this book's rituals can work with children.

Cunningham, Scott and David Harrington. *The Magical Household*. St. Paul, MN: Llewellyn Publications, 1987. Concerned more with the craft of Wicca than the religion. It has good sections on the seasons, garden, altars, and household protection.

Danaher, Kevin. *The Year in Ireland*. 4th ed. St. Paul, MN: Irish Books and Media, 1972. Seasonal customs in Ireland. Belongs in every Celtophile's library.

_____ . "Irish Folk Tradition and the Celtic Calendar," *The Celtic Consciousness*. Ed. by Robert O'Driscoll. New York: George Braziller, 1981.

Danielli, Mary. "Inititiation Ceremonial from Norse Literature," *Folklore* 56:2 June 1945, pp. 229-45.

Dass, Ram. *Be Here Now*. Boulder, CO: Hanuman Foundation, 1978. Written mostly from a Hindu or general mystical point of view. Contains advice on family spiritual practice.

DeGidio, Sandra. *Enriching Faith Through Family Celebrations*. Mystic, CT: Twenty-Third Publications, 1989. Written from a Christian point of view. Has many good suggestions, particularly on seasonal celebrations.

Early Irish Myths and Sagas. Trans. by Jeffrey Gantz. Harmondsworth, U.K.: Penguin, 1981.

Eliade, Mircea. *Myths, Dreams, and Mysteries*. London: Harvill Press, 1960.

_____ . *Rites and Symbols of Initiation*. New York: Harper and Row, 1958. Includes information on puberty rites.

_____ . *The Sacred and the Profane*. Trans. by Willard R. Trask. New York: Harcourt Brace Jovanovich, 1959. Classic treatment of sacred time and space. Information on temples, homes, and rites of passage. Very readable and highly recommended.

Farrar, Janet and Stewart. *Eight Sabbats for Witches*. London: Robert Hale, 1981. A lot of information on seasonal customs and beliefs, baby blessing, handfasting, and funeral.

_____ . *The Witches' Goddess*. Washington, DC: Phoenix Publishing, 1987.

Fitch, Ed. *Magical Rites from the Crystal Well*. St. Paul, MN: Llewellyn Publications, 1984. Includes seasonal rituals, baby blessing, handfasting, divorce, and funeral.

_____ . *The Rites of Odin*. St. Paul, MN: Llewellyn Publications, 1990. Norse Neo-Pagans have done well integrating their religions and their families. Contains seasonal rituals, betrothal, wedding, birth pledging, coming of age, divorce, and funeral.

Fitzpatrick, Jean Grasso. *Something More: Nurturing Your Child's Spiritual Growth*. New York: Viking Penguin, 1991. Mostly Judeo-Christian, but still useful.

Foster, Steven and Meredith Little. *The Book of the Vision Quest*. New York: Prentice Hall Press, 1988. Accounts of vision quests, with valuable information for those who wish to make a safe one.

_____ . *The Roaring of the Sacred River: The Wilderness Quest for Vision and Self-Healing*. New York: Prentice Hall Press, 1989. Particularly useful for those who wish to help others make their vision quest.

Frazer, Sir James. *The New Golden Bough*. Ed. by Theodore Gaster. New York: New American Library, 1959. Although his conclusions have been rejected by anthropology, this is still a good source of folk customs.

Funk & Wagnall Standard Dictionary of Folklore, Mythology, and Legend. Ed. by Maria Leach. San Fransisco, CA: Harper & Row, 1972. A must for anyone interested in folk customs.

Gaster, Theodor H. *Festivals of the Jewish Year*. New York: William Sloane, 1953. In discussing the traditions of Jewish celebrations, he gives many customs from other traditions.

Green, Marian. *A Calendar of Festivals: Traditional Celebrations, Songs, Seasonal Recipes, and Things to Make*. Rockport, Massachusetts: Element, Inc., 1991. Wonderful suggestions for seasonal observance. Two warnings, though. First, the recipes are written for a British audience and may need some translation. She writes "jelly" where we would say "gelatin," for instance. Second, while her reporting of ancient customs is generally spot on, the explanations and etymologies she gives for them are frequently in error or are speculation rather than fact. Used carefully, this is a welcome addition to anyone's library.

Grimal, Pierre. *The Civilization of Rome*. New York: Simon & Schuster, 1963.

Hutton, Ronald. *The Pagan Religions of the Ancient British Isles*. Cambridge, MA: Basil Blackwell, 1991. Useful information on pre-Christian calendars. Much information from the last twenty years of archaeology, usually missing from Neo-Pagan writings. A must-read for all Neo-Pagans.

James, Edwin Oliver. *Seasonal Feasts and Festivals*. Norwich, U.K. Prehistoric, Egyptian, Mesopotamian, Palestinian, Anatolian, Greek, Roman, and European Christian seasonal celebrations.

Klein, Tzipora. *Celebrating Life: Rites of Passage for All Ages*. Oak Park, IL: Delphi Press, Inc., 1992. Wiccaning, puberty, new home, betrothal, wedding, divorce, and funeral rituals.

Lewis, I.M. *Ecstatic Religion: An Anthropological Study of Spirit Possession and Shamanism*. Harmondsworth, U.K.: Penguin Books, Ltd., 1971.

Lincoln, Bruce. *Emerging from the Chrysalis: Studies in Rituals of Women's Initiations*. Cambridge, MA: Harvard University, 1981. Analysis by a historian of religion of female coming of age rites in five cultures, plus a discussion of such rites in general.

Linke, Uli. "Blood as Metaphor in Proto-Indo-European," *Journal of Indo-European Studies* 12:3 and 4 1985, pp. 333-375.

Llewellyn's Magical Almanac. St. Paul, MN: Llewellyn Publications. Published annually. Lists festivals from many traditions. Includes articles by a variety of authors on folk customs, magic, and ritual.

MacCana, Proinsias. *Celtic Mythology*. New York: Hamlyn Publishing Group, 1970.

MacNeill, Maire. "The Musician in the Cave," *Bealoideas* 57 1989, pp. 109-32. A treatment of Lughnasad customs and folklore.

McCarroll, Tolbert. *Guiding God's Children*. New York: Paulist Press, 1983. Written from a Christian point of view by a monk. Strongly influenced by Zen Buddhism, the emphasis is on spirituality and nature.

McNeill, F. Marian. *The Silver Bough*. 4 vols. Glasgow: William Mac-Clellan, 1959. Folk customs from Scotland. Should be read by anyone interested in Celtic cultures.

Montgomery, Rita E. "A Cross-Cultural Study of Menstruation, Menstrual Taboos, and Related Social Variables," *Ethos* 2:2 Summer 1974, pp. 137-70.

Newall, Venetia. "Easter Eggs," *Journal of American Folklore* 80 1967, pp. 3-32. Not just about Easter and not just American; egg myths and customs from around the world regarding birth, weddings, funerals, May Day, Harvest, and planting.

Newman, Dana. *The Complete Teacher's Almanack: A Practical Guide to All Twelve Months of the Year*. West Nyack, NY: The Center for Applied Research in Education, 1991. Seasonal, holiday, environmental, and Native American activities for young children.

Ni Padraiga, Macha and the New York Reconstructed Celtic Folk Church. *Brighid's Day*. Unpublished manuscript, 1986.

Ono, Sokyo. *Shinto: The Kami Way*. Rutland, VT: Charles E. Tuttle Company, 1972. Shinto, the folk religion of Japan, is the only form of Paganism that has survived to this day in an industrialized culture, and thus it has much to teach us. It is especially useful in researching household shrines, offerings, and ancestor worship.

Plutarch. *The Roman Questions of Plutarch*. Trans. by H.J. Rose. New York: Biblo and Tannen, 1974.

Polome, Edgar C. "Germanic Religion and the Indo-European Heritage," *Mankind Quarterly* 26:1 and 2 Fall/Winter 1985, pp. 27-55.

Posch, S. "Can Paganism find Happiness in the Big City?" *The Crystal Well* 14:2 1981, p. 29.

Quintero, Nita. "Coming of Age the Apache Way," *National Geographic* 157:2 February 1980, pp. 262-71.

Raphael, Roy. *The Men from the Boys: Rites of Passage in Male America*. Lincoln, Nebraska: University of Nebraska Press, 1988.

Robbins, Miriam E. *Indo-European Female Figures*. Dissertation, UCLA, 1978. Ann Arbor, MI: University Microfilms International, 1979.

_____ . "The Assimilation of Pre-Indo-European Goddesses into Indo-European Society," *Journal of Indo-European Studies* 7:1 and 2 Spring/ Summer 1980, pp. 19-29.

Rose, H.J. *Ancient Roman Religion*. London: Cheltenham Press, 1948.

The Sacred Pipe. Ed. by Joseph Epes Brown. Harmondsworth, U.K.: Penguin Books, 1971. The seven rites of the Oglala Sioux. Includes directions for sweat lodges, vision quests, and girl's puberty rite.

Scullard, H.H. *Festivals and Ceremonies of the Roman Republic*. London: Thames and Hudson, 1981. Description of general Roman religious practices, followed by a calendar of the many holidays of the Romans.

Squire, Charles. *Celtic Myth and Legend*. Hollywood, CA: Newcastle Publishing, 1975.

Starhawk. *The Spiral Dance: A Rebirth of the Ancient Religion of the Great Goddess*. 2nd ed. New York: HarperCollins, 1989.

Syme, Daniel B. *The Jewish Home*. New York: UAHC Press, 1988. Especially useful for Judeo-Pagans, but can be used by anyone looking for living traditions.

Van Gennep, Arnold. *The Rites of Passage*. London: Routledge & Kegan Paul, 1960. Classic work that introduced the term "rite of passage." Includes information on coming of age, birth, weddings, and funerals.

Volpe, Angel Della. "From the Hearth to the Creation of Boundaries," *Journal of Indo-European Studies* 18:1 and 2 1990, pp. 157-84. Information primarily on hearths, but also sacred space, weddings, and births.

_____ . "On Indo-European Ceremonial and Socio-Political Elements Underlying the Origin of Formal Boundaries," _Journal of Indo-European Studies_, 20:1 and 2 Spring/Summer 1992, pp. 71-122. Packed with information on the domestic cults of the various Indo-European peoples. Don't let the title scare you.

Wolfe, Amber. _In the Shadow of the Shaman_. St. Paul, MN: Llewellyn Publications, 1988. Contains exercises for awakening awareness of the spiritual side of nature.

Children's Books

These are books that can either be read by or to children. The suggested ages are based on the books being read by the children themselves; if you are going to be reading them out loud, they can be enjoyed by younger children.

Arthen, Deirdre Pulgram. _Walking With Mother Earth_. West Boxford, MA: D & J Publications, 1992. Ages 5-10. Originally intended as a guided meditation about the Goddess and the God, it has been adapted into story form.

The Earthworks Group. _Fifty Simple Things Kids Can Do to Save the Earth_. Kansas City, MO: Andrews and McMeed, 1990. The title says it all.

Frost, Robert. _Stopping by Woods on a Snowy Evening_. New York: E. P. Dutton, 1978. Ages 4-10. Illustrated (by Susan Jeffers) version of a poem that takes place on Yule, in which the poet may be seen as the sun stopping in the darkness before continuing on his way. A reading of this poem is a Yule tradition in my family.

Goble, Paul. _The Gift of the Sacred Dog_. New York: MacMillan Publishing Co., 1980. Ages 4-7. Plains Indian story of the coming of the horse.

Grahame, Kenneth. _The Wind in the Willows_. New York: Dell Publishing Co., 1969. The language is quite difficult, so a child will have to be nine or older to read it herself, but you don't want to wait that long. Read it to your children with some editing as you do. Of special interest is Chapter 7, "The Piper at the Gates of Dawn," an encounter with Pan. This book is published in a number of editions by different publishers.

Grimm, Jacob and Wilhelm. *The Complete Fairy Tales of the Brothers Grimm*. Trans. by Jack Zipes. New York: Bantam Books, 1988. This two volume collection has all of the Grimm's fairy tales, unabridged. It has, of course, "Iron Hans," made so famous by Robert Bly. The age at which these are appropriate will vary with the tale, so you will need to read them first.

Hallinan, P.K. *For the Love of Our Earth*. Nashville, TN: Ideas Publishing Co., 1992. Ages 3-5. A poem designed to inspire children to care for the Earth and each other.

Hyer, Carol. *The Whale's Song*. New York: Dial Books, 1991. Ages 4-6. A girl learns through whales that nature is here for its own purpose, not ours.

Mayer, Marianna. *Noble-Hearted Kate*. New York: Bantam Doubleday Dell Publishing Group, 1990. Ages 8-10. An original tale, based on Celtic folklore, of Kate, who saves both her stepsister and a prince, on "the Eve of Samhain when the veil between the realm of Faerie and the realm of man is drawn apart and anything can happen."

Parramon, J.M. *The Four Elements*. Ages 8-10. Hauppauge, NY: Barron's Educational Series, 1985. A set of four books, sometimes sold separately, describing the elements.

Phelps, Ethel Johnston. *The Maid of the North: Feminist Folk Tales from Around the World*. New York: Henry Holt and Co., 1981. Fairy tales in which the hero is a heroine. Different tales are appropriate for different ages. Contains the story of Gawain and Lady Ragnell.

Sanderson, Ruth. *The Enchanted World*. Boston, MA: Little, Brown, and Co., 1991. Ages 5-9. Helped by a maiden, a prince saves his land which has been in drought since the death of its queen.

Tresselt, Alvin. *The Gift of the Tree*. New York: Lothrop, Lee, and Shepard Books, 1992. Ages 4-8. The story of a rotting oak tree and the gift of life it gives to the forest.

White Deer of Autumn. *Ceremony: In the Circle of Life*. Hillsboro, OR: Beyond Words Publishing, Inc., 1981. Ages 5-10. A Native American boy living in the city is visited by a spirit guide who teaches him his people's ways.

Recordings

Chameleon and Friends. *A Bardic Circle*. Cleveland Heights, OH: Association for Consciousness Exploration, 1988. Contains "He is Reborn," by Bert Talm, a lovely Yule song.

Corrigan, Ian. *Once Around the Wheel: Modern and Traditional Seasonal Songs*. Cleveland Heights, OH: Association for Consciousness Exploration, 1987. Recorded at a workshop. Includes seasonal songs and discussion of customs.

Folk Songs of Britain, Vol. IX: Songs of Ceremony. Ed. by Peter Kennedy and Alan Lormax. London: Topic Records, Ltd., 1961. Seasonal songs, including May carols, "John Barleycorn," and Wassailing songs.

Jethro Tull. *Songs from the Wood*. Los Angeles, CA: Chrysalis, 1977. Includes a May song and a Yule song.

Pendderwen, Gwydion. *Songs for the Old Religion*. Oakland, CA: Nemeton, 1975. Pagan songs, mostly seasonal.

Steeleye Span. *Below the Salt*. Ho-Ho-Kus, NJ: Shanachie, 1984. Contains the most accessible version of "John Barleycorn."

Index

Stay in Touch

On the following pages you will find listed, with their current prices, some of the books now available on related subjects. Your book dealer stocks most of these and will stock new titles in the Llewellyn series as they become available. We urge your patronage.

To obtain our full catalog, to keep informed about new titles as they are released and to benefit from informative articles and helpful news, you are invited to write for our bimonthly news magazine/catalog, *Llewellyn's New Worlds of Mind and Spirit*. A sample copy is free, and it will continue coming to you at no cost as long as you are an active mail customer. Or you may subscribe for just $10.00 in the U.S.A. and Canada ($20.00 overseas, first class mail). Many bookstores also have New Worlds available to their customers. Ask for it.

Stay in touch! In *New Worlds'* pages you will find news and features about new books, tapes and services, announcements of meetings and seminars, articles helpful to our readers, news of authors, products and services, special money-making opportunities, and much more.

Llewellyn's New Worlds of Mind and Spirit
P.O. Box 64383-210, St. Paul, MN 55164-0383, U.S.A.
* * *

To Order Books and Tapes

If your book dealer does not have the books described on the following page readily available, you may order them directly from the publisher by sending full price in U.S. funds, plus $3.00 for postage and handling for orders under $10.00; $4.00 for orders over $10.00. There are no postage and handling charges for orders over $50.00. Postage and handling rates are subject to change. UPS Delivery: We ship UPS whenever possible. Delivery guaranteed. Provide your street address as UPS does not deliver to P.O. Boxes. Allow 4-6 weeks for delivery. UPS to Canada requires a $50.00 minimum order. Orders outside the U.S.A. and Canada: airmail—add retail price of book; add $5.00 for each non-book item (tapes, etc.); add $1.00 per item for surface mail.

For Group Study and Purchase

Because there is a great deal of interest in group discussion and study of the subject matter of this book, we feel that we should encourage the adoption and use of this particular book by such groups by offering a special quantity price to group leaders or agents. Our special quantity price for a minimum order of five copies of *The Pagan Family* is $38.85 cash-with-order. This price includes postage and handling within the United States. Minnesota residents must add 6.5% sales tax. For additional quantities, please order in multiples of five. For Canadian and foreign orders, add postage and handling charges as above. Credit card (VISA, Master-Card, American Express) orders are accepted. Charge card orders only ($15.00 minimum order) may be phoned in free within the U.S.A. or Canada by dialing 1-800-THE-MOON. For customer service, call 1-612-291-1970. Mail orders to:

LLEWELLYN PUBLICATIONS
P.O. Box 64383-210, St. Paul, MN 55164-0383, U.S.A.

Prices subject to change without notice.

THE FAMILY WICCA BOOK
The Craft for Parents & Children
by Ashleen O'Gaea

Enjoy the first book written for Pagan parents! The number of Witches raising children to the Craft is growing. The need for mutual support is rising—yet until now, there have been no books that speak to a Wiccan family's needs and experience. Finally, here is *The Family Wicca Book*, full to the brim with rituals, projects, encouragement, and practical discussion of real-life challenges. You'll find lots of ideas to use right away.

Is magic safe for children? Why do some people think Wiccans are Satanists? How do you make friends with spirits and little people in the local woods? Find out how one Wiccan family gives clear and honest answers to questions that intrigue pagans all over the world.

When you want to ground your family in Wicca without ugly "bashing;" explain life, sex, and death without embarrassment; and add to your Sabbats without much trouble or expense, *The Family Wicca Book* is required reading. You'll refer to it again and again as your traditions grow with your family.

0-87542-591-7, 240 pgs., 5-1/4 x 8, illus., softcover **$9.95**

WHEEL OF THE YEAR
Living the Magical Life
by Pauline Campanelli, illustrated by Dan Campanelli

If you feel elated by the celebrations of the Sabbats and hunger for that feeling during the long weeks between Sabbats, *Wheel of the Year* can help you put the joy and fulfillment of magic into your everyday life. This book shows you how to celebrate the lesser changes in Nature. The wealth of seasonal rituals and charms are all easily performed with materials readily available and are simple and concise enough that the practitioner can easily adapt them to work within the framework of his or her own Pagan tradition.

Learn to perform fire magic in November, the secret Pagan symbolism of Christmas tree ornaments, the best time to visit a fairy forest or sacred spring and what to do when you get there. Learn the charms and rituals and the making of magical tools that coincide with the nesting season of migratory birds. Whether you are a newcomer to the Craft or have found your way back many years ago, *Wheel of the Year* will be an invaluable reference book in your practical magic library. It is filled with magic and ritual for everyday life and will enhance any system of Pagan ritual.

0-87542-091-5, 176 pgs., 7 x 10, illus., softcover **$9.95**

ANCIENT WAYS
Reclaiming the Pagan Tradition
by Pauline Campanelli, illustrated by Dan Campanelli

Ancient Ways is filled with magic and ritual that you can perform every day to capture the spirit of the seasons. It focuses on the celebration of the Sabbats of the Old Religion by giving you practical things to do while anticipating the Sabbat rites, and helping you harness the magical energy for weeks afterward. The wealth of seasonal rituals and charms are drawn from ancient sources but are easily performed with materials readily available.

Learn how to look into your previous lives at Yule … at Beltane, discover the places where you are most likely to see faeries … make special jewelry to wear for your Lammas celebrations … for the special animals in your life, paint a charm of protection at Midsummer.

Most Pagans and Wiccans feel that the Sabbat rituals are all too brief and wish for the magic to linger on. *Ancient Ways* can help you reclaim your own traditions and heighten the feeling of magic.

0-87542-090-7, 256 pgs., 7 x 10, illus., softcover   **$12.95**

CIRCLES, GROVES & SANCTUARIES
Sacred Spaces of Today's Pagans
compiled by Dan and Pauline Campanelli

Pagans and Wiccans have always been secretive people. Even many within the Craft have not been allowed to enter the sacred space of others. But within the pages of *Circles, Groves & Sanctuaries*, you are given the unique opportunity to examine, in intimate detail, the magical places created by Pagans and Witches across the country, around the world, and from a wide variety of traditions.

Take guided tours of sacred spaces by the people who created them, and listen as they tell of the secret meanings and magical symbolism of the sometimes strange and always wonderful objects that adorn these places. Learn of their rituals that can be adapted by the most seasoned practitioner or the newest seeker on the hidden path. Become inspired to create your own magical space—indoors or out, large or small.

Accompany an Irish Count on a vision quest that led to the creation of a shrine to Poseidon. Read of the Celtic-speaking Fairies who dwell and practice their arts in Florida, and learn of the logistics of building a wood-henge in suburban New Jersey and a stone circle in the heart of the Bible Belt.

0-87542-108-3, 288 pgs., 7 x 10, 120 photos, softcover   **$12.95**

Prices subject to change without notice.

WICCA
A Guide for the Solitary Practitioner
by Scott Cunningham

Wicca is a book of life and how to live magically, spiritually, and wholly attuned with Nature. It is a book of sense and common sense, not only about magic, but about religion and one of the most critical issues of today: how to achieve the much needed and wholesome relationship with out Earth. Cunningham presents Wicca as it is today: a gentle, Earth-oriented religion dedicated to the Goddess and God. This book fulfills a need for a practical guide to solitary Wicca—a need which no previous book has fulfilled.

Here is a positive, practical introduction to the religion of Wicca, designed so that any interested person can learn to practice the religion alone, anywhere in the world. It presents Wicca honestly and clearly, without the pseudo-history that permeates other books. It shows that Wicca is a vital, satisfying part of twentieth-century life.

0-87542-118-0, 240 pgs., 6 x 9, illus., softcover $9.95

LIVING WICCA
A Further Guide for the Solitary Practitioner
by Scott Cunningham

Living Wicca is the long-awaited sequel to Scott Cunningham's wildly successful *Wicca: A Guide for the Solitary Practitioner*. This new book is for those who have made the conscious decision to bring their Wiccan spirituality into their everyday lives. It provides solitary practitioners with the tools and added insights that will enable them to blaze their own spiritual paths—to become their own high priests and priestesses.

Living Wicca takes a philosophical look at the questions, practices, and differences within Witchcraft. It covers the various tools of learning available to the practitioner, the importance of secrecy in one's practice, guidelines to performing ritual when ill, magical names, initiation, and the Mysteries. It discusses the benefits of daily prayer and meditation, making offerings to the gods, how to develop a prayerful attitude, and how to perform Wiccan rites when away from home or in emergency situations.

Unlike any other book on the subject, *Living Wicca* is a step-by-step guide to creating your own Wiccan tradition and personal vision of the gods, designing your personal ritual and symbols, developing your own book of shadows, and truly living your Craft.

0-87542-184-9, 208 pgs., 6 x 9, illus., softcover $10.00

CUNNINGHAM'S ENCYCLOPEDIA OF MAGICAL HERBS
by Scott Cunningham
This is the most comprehensive source of herbal data for magical uses ever printed! Almost every one of the over 400 herbs are illustrated, making this a great source for herb identification. For each herb you will also find: magical properties, planetary rulerships, genders, associated deities, folk and Latin names, and much more. To make this book even easier to use, it contains a folk name cross reference, and all of the herbs are fully indexed. There is also a large annotated bibliography and a list of mail order suppliers so you can find the books and herbs you need.

Like all of Cunningham's books, this one does not require you to use complicated rituals or expensive magical paraphernalia. Instead, it shares with you the intrinsic powers of the herbs. Thus, you will be able to discover which herbs, by their very nature, can be used for luck, love, success, money, divination, astral projection, safety, psychic self-defense, and much more.

Besides being interesting and educational it is also fun and fully illustrated with unusual woodcuts from old herbals. This book has rapidly become the classic in its field. It enhances books such as *777* and is a must for all Wiccans.

0-87542-122-9, 336 pgs., 6 x 9, illus., softcover   **$12.95**

THE MAGIC IN FOOD
Legends, Lore & Spells
by Scott Cunningham
Foods are storehouses of natural energies. Choosing specific foods, properly preparing them, eating with a magical goal in mind: these are the secrets of *The Magic in Food*, an age-old method of taking control of your life through your diet.

Though such exotic dishes as bird's-nest soup and saffron bread are included in this book, you'll find many old friends: peanut butter and jelly sandwiches ... scrambled eggs ... tofu ... beer. We've consumed them for years, but until we're aware of the energies contained within them, foods offer little more than nourishment and pleasure.

You'll learn the mystic qualities of everyday dishes, their preparation (if any) and the simple method of calling upon their powers. The author has included numerous magical diets, each designed to create a specific change within its user: increased health and happiness, deeper spirituality, enhanced sexual relations, protection, psychic awareness, success, love, prosperity—all through the hidden powers of food.

0-87542-130-X, 384 pgs., 6 x 9, illus., color plates, softcover   **$14.95**

THE MAGICAL HOUSEHOLD
Empower Your Home with Love, Protection, Health and Happiness
by Scott Cunningham and David Harrington
Whether your home is a small apartment or a palatial mansion, you want it to be something special. Now it can be with *The Magical Household*. Learn how to make your home more than just a place to live. Turn it into a place of security, life, fun, and magic. Here you will not find the complex magic of the ceremonial magician. Rather, you will learn simple, quick, and effective magical spells that use nothing more than common items in your house: furniture, windows, doors, carpet, pets, etc. You will learn to take advantage of the intrinsic power and energy that is already in your home, waiting to be tapped. You will learn to make magic a part of your life. The result is a home that is safeguarded from harm and a place which will bring you happiness, health, and more.
0-87542-124-5, 208 pgs., 5-1/4 x 8, illus., softcover　　　　**$8.95**

SPELL CRAFTS
Creating Magical Objects
by Scott Cunningham and David Harrington
Since early times, crafts have been intimately linked with spirituality. When a woman carefully shaped a water jar from the clay she'd gathered from a river bank, she was performing a spiritual practice. When crafts were used to create objects intended for ritual or that symbolized the Divine, the connection between the craftsperson and divinity grew more intense. Today, handcrafts can still be more than a pastime—they can be rites of power and honor; a religious ritual. After all, hands were our first magical tools.

Spell Crafts is a modern guide to creating physical objects for the attainment of specific magical goals. It is far different from magic books that explain how to use purchased magical tools. You will learn how to fashion spell brooms, weave wheat, dip candles, sculpt clay, mix herbs, bead sacred symbols, and much more, for a variety of purposes. Whatever your craft, you will experience the natural process of moving energy from within yourself (or within natural objects) to create positive change.
0-87542-185-7, 224 pgs., 5-1/4 x 8, illus., photos　　　　**$10.00**

IN THE SHADOW OF THE SHAMAN
Connecting with Self, Nature & Spirit
by Amber Wolfe

Presented in what the author calls a "cookbook shamanism style," this book shares recipes, ingredients, and methods of preparation for experiencing some very ancient wisdoms: wisdoms of Native American and Wiccan traditions, as well as contributions from other philosophies of Nature as they are used in the shamanic way. Wheels, the circle, totems, shields, directions, divinations, spells, care of sacred tools, and meditations are all discussed. Amber Wolfe encourages us to feel confident and free to use her methods to cook up something new, completely on our own. This blending of ancient formulas and personal methods represents what she calls Aquarian Shamanism.

In the Shadow of the Shaman is designed to communicate in the most practical, direct ways possible, so that the wisdom and the energy may be shared for the benefits of all. Whatever your system or tradition, you will find this to be a valuable book, a resource, a friend, a gentle guide and support on your journey. Dancing in the shadow of the shaman, you will find new dimensions of Spirit.

0-87542-888-6, 384 pgs., 6 x 9, illus., softcover **$12.95**

CHARMS, SPELLS & FORMULAS
For the Making and Use of Gris-Gris Bags, Herb Candles, Doll Magic, Incenses, Oils and Powders
by Ray Malbrough

Hoodoo magic is a blend of European techniques and the magic brought to the New World by slaves from Africa. Now you can learn the methods which have been used successfully by Hoodoo practitioners for nearly 200 years.

By using the simple materials available in nature, you can bring about the necessary changes to greatly benefit your life and that of your friends. You are given detailed instructions for making and using the "gris-gris" (charm) bags only casually or mysteriously mentioned by other writers. Malbrough not only shows how to make gris-gris bags for health, money, luck, love, and protection from evil and harm, but he also explains how these charms work. He also takes you into the world of doll magic to gain love, success, or prosperity. Complete instructions are given for making the dolls and setting up the ritual.

0-87542-501-1, 192 pgs., 5-1/4 x 8, illus., softcover **$6.95**

Prices subject to change without notice.

LLEWELLYN'S MAGICAL ALMANAC

This enchanting yearly guide for Pagans has become a faithful friend to magical people the world over. It's chock full of articles, usable monthly calendars, magical advice, and captivating artwork. What's more, its value lasts beyond the year—the captivating articles on a variety of magical subjects make this a long-cherished keepsake for decades to come.

288 pgs., 5-1/4 x 8, softcover   **State year $7.95**

THE MAGICAL DIARY
A Personal Ritual Journal
by Donald Michael Kraig

Virtually every teacher of magic, whether it is a book or an individual, will advise you to keep a record of your magical rituals. Unfortunately, most people keep these records in a collection of different sized and different looking books, frequently forgetting to include important data. *The Magical Diary* changes this forever. In this book are pages waiting to be filled in. Each page has headings for all of the important information including date, time, astrological information, planetary hour, name of rituals performed, results, comments, and much more. Use some of them or use them all. This book was specially designed to be perfect for all magicians no matter what tradition you are involved in. Everybody who does magic needs *The Magical Diary*.

0-87542-322-1, 240 pgs., 7 x 8 1/2, otabound   **$9.95**

PLAYFUL MAGIC
by Janina Renee

A carefree, playful spirit appears to be the key to an enchanted existence. Light-hearted people are genuinely luckier, and all aspects of life just seem to work better for them. Expressing the playful self, which includes nourishing the "inner child," brings spiritual and emotional enrichment. Many psychological and metaphysical systems emphasize that our playful self is connected to our personal vitality, our intuition, and the unified state of mind and being that puts us in sync with the life pulse of the universe.

Playful Magic is a "how to" book that provides magical techniques for helping your life run more smoothly. It is a collection of meditations, visualizations, magical exercises, suggestions, and philosophy aimed at taking you outside of yourself and away from worries and problems. It shows you how to recover that special quality of energy that seems to be the source, the essence of life. *Playful Magic* will help you remember that magic isn't separate from the routines of daily life—it in fact permeates all existence. To integrate magic into life is not to trivialize the deeper mysteries, but to make the mystery of living more meaningful.

0-87542-678-6, 288 pgs., 6 x 9, 50 illus., softcover   **$12.95**

MAGICAL RITES FROM THE CRYSTAL WELL
by Ed Fitch

In nature, and in the earth, we look and find beauty. Within ourselves we find a well from which we may draw truth and knowledge. And when we draw from this well, we rediscover that we are all children of the Earth.

The simple rites in this book are presented to you as a means of finding your own way back to nature; for discovering and experiencing the beauty and the magic of unity with the source. These are the celebrations of the seasons; at the same time they are rites by which we attune ourselves to the flow of the force: the energy of life.

These are rites of passage by which we celebrate the major transitions we all experience in life. Here are the Old Ways, but they are also the Ways for Today.

0-87542-230-6, 160 pgs., 7 x 10, illus., softcover **$9.95**

THE RITES OF ODIN
by Ed Fitch

The ancient Northern Europeans knew a rough magic drawn from the grandeur of vast mountains and deep forests, of rolling oceans and thundering storms. Their rites and beliefs sustained the Vikings, accompanying them to the New World and to the Steppes of Central Asia. Now, for the first time, this magic system is brought compellingly into the present by author Ed Fitch.

This is a complete source volume on Odinism. It stresses the ancient values as well as the magic and myth of this way of life. The author researched his material in Scandinavia and Germany, and drew from anthropological and historical sources in Eastern and Central Europe.

A full cycle of ritual is provided, with rites of passage, magical spells, divination techniques, and three sets of seasonal rituals: solitary, group, and family. *The Rites of Odin* also contains extensive "how-to" sections on planning and conducting Odinist ceremonies, including preparation of ceremonial implements and the setting up of ritual areas. Each section is designed to stand alone for easier reading and for quick reference. A bibliography is provided for those who wish to pursue the historical and anthropological roots of Odinism further.

0-87542-224-1, 360 pgs., 6 x 9, illus., softcover **$12.95**